How Games Move Us

Playful Thinking

Jesper Juul, Geoffrey Long, and William Uricchio, editors

The Art of Failure: An Essay on the Pain of Playing Video Games, Jesper Juul, 2013

Uncertainty in Games, Greg Costikyan, 2013

Play Matters, Miguel Sicart, 2014

Works of Game: On the Aesthetics of Games and Art, John Sharp, 2015

How Games Move Us: Emotion by Design, Katherine Isbister, 2016

How Games Move Us

Emotion by Design

Katherine Isbister

The MIT Press
Cambridge, Massachusetts
London, England

First MIT Press paperback edition, 2017

This book was set in Stone Sans Std and Stone Serif Std by Toppan Best-set Premedia. Printed and bound in the United States of America.

Library of Congress Cataloging-in-Publication Data

Names: Isbister, Katherine.
Title: How games move us : emotion by design / Katherine Isbister.
Description: Cambridge, MA : MIT Press, 2016. | Series: Playful thinking | Includes bibliographical references and index.
Identifiers: LCCN 2015038398 | ISBN 9780262034265 (hardcover : alk. paper) | 9780262534451 (pb.)
Subjects: LCSH: Video games--Design. | Video games--Psychological aspects. | Computer games--Psychological aspects.
Classification: LCC GV1469.3 .K38 2016 | DDC 794.8--dc23 LC record available at http://lccn.loc.gov/2015038398

10   9   8

This book is dedicated to my stepfather Anthony Falcone, who has been an enduring and devoted fan—ever willing to lend an ear, send a reference, and in general cheerlead the myriad efforts that are necessary to get such a project done. And also, to my Ph.D. advisor Clifford Nass, a brilliant, enthusiastic mentor who is sorely missed.

Contents

On Thinking Playfully

Many people (we series editors included) find video games exhilarating, but it can be just as interesting to ponder why that is so. What do video games do? What can they be used for? How do they work? How do they relate to the rest of the world? Why is play both so important and so powerful?

Playful Thinking is a series of short, readable, and argumentative books that share some playfulness and excitement with the games that they are about. Each book in the series is small enough to fit in a backpack or coat pocket, and combines depth with readability for any reader interested in playing more thoughtfully or thinking more playfully. This includes, but is by no means limited to, academics, game makers, and curious players.

So, we are casting our net wide. Each book in our series provides a blend of new insights and interesting arguments with overviews of knowledge from game studies and other areas. You will see this reflected not just in the range of titles in our series, but in the range of authors creating them. Our basic assumption is simple: video games are such a flourishing medium that any new perspective on them is likely to show us something unseen or forgotten, including those from such unconventional voices as artists, philosophers, or specialists in other industries or fields of study. These books are bridge builders, cross-pollinating areas with both new knowledge and new ways of thinking.

At its heart, this is what Playful Thinking is all about: new ways of thinking about games and new ways of using games to think about the rest of the world.

Jesper Juul
Geoffrey Long
William Uricchio

Acknowledgments

The writing of this humble tome took a surprising amount of time and effort. Thanks to the Humboldt Foundation, and Marc Alexa of Technische Universität Berlin, for supporting me through multiple summers of writing. Thanks to the CASBS Center at Stanford University for supporting me during the sabbatical year that brought the writing all the way to completion (and to the Annenberg Fund for fellowship support). While at Stanford, I benefited from presenting and discussing these ideas with students of Michael Bernstein and James Landay in the HCI program, with attendees of the Games and Interactive Media lecture series put together by Henry Lowood, Ingmar Riedel-Kruse, Sebastian Alvarado, Paul Zenke, Chris Bennett, and colleagues; with attendees of the Media-X annual conference hosted by Martha Russell; with Karin Forssell and her students in the Learning, Design, and Technology master's program; and with the fabulous Wendy Ju. There were of course lively conversations with fellow CASBS fellows, who gave me much sage advice, and a fun title brainstorm with Scott Bukatman.

Thanks to New York University for providing me a scholarly home base over these years. The Game Innovation Lab was a wonderful incubator for research on games and emotion. Terrific colleagues from the Game Engineering group in the Computer Science Department and from the NYU Game Center influenced how I think about games and what they do for us. Discussing games as a cultural form with Frank Lantz, Eric Zimmerman, Jesper Juul, and other early Game Center community members particularly shaped my own thinking about the framing of this book.

Much appreciation to those who read over drafts and discussed the ideas herein with me: Kaho Abe, Gabriella Etmektsoglou, Clara Fernandez-Vara, Michael Mateas, Andy Nealen, Syed Salahuddin, Fred Turner, Sharra Vostral; and the graduate students who I have had the privilege to work with on these themes over the last few years—Xiaofeng Chen, Jonathan Frye, Chelsea Hash, Michael Karlesky, Shoshana Kessock, Suzanne Kirkpatrick, Elena Márquez Segura, Edward Melcer, Shilpan Patel, Toni Pizza, Rahul Rao, Holly Robbins, Ulf Schwekendiek, Raybit Tang, and Kong Tsao (and many more who I inadvertently omitted, I'm sure—please forgive me!). And thanks to Chrystanyaa Brown and Chris DiMauro for keeping the lab going so we could all build great research games there.

Thanks to those in the game development community who have explored the intersection of game design and emotion with their games, writings, and public presentations. In particular, the work of Jenova Chen and Nicole Lazzaro has been influential to me, and their efforts are cited in these pages.

Thanks to the series editors and those at the MIT Press who shepherded this book along, in particular Jesper Juul, my erstwhile colleague at NYU and my patient editor, and Doug Sery, who has been a tireless champion of thoughtful writing on games. Thanks to Christine Larson for her adept amendment of my turgid academic tone, and to Luke Stark for tidying references and gathering image permissions. Thanks to Kristina Höök for hosting me and egging me on while I made and uploaded the final changes to the manuscript.

Finally, on the home front, a shout-out to my husband, Rene Netter, who is always game to listen to an idea that trails me home from work, and to my daughter Nona Lily Netter, who keeps my life playful.

Introduction

Games have reached a watershed moment in our culture. Pretty much everyone now accepts the fact that games are a big deal—a huge revenue generator with sales in the same league as film and books, and a daily presence in the lives of millions of people in one form or another. We collect games in museums and read about them in high culture venues like the *New York Times*. But the public conversation around games isn't as nuanced and well informed as it could be, and really, as it *needs* to be.

To have a rich and meaningful discussion about how games fit into our lives, how they work on us as human beings, we need to get beyond shadowboxing with a monolithic notion of "games," and delve into the elements that make up the game experience in all its facets. We would never lump Hollywood action films, Sundance winners, and nature documentaries together when discussing the impact of film. We see these as different kinds of works, using different techniques, for different audiences, to different ends. We don't hold films from each of these categories to the same standards as the others. We wouldn't assume Hollywood films represent the full emotional register of filmmaking, and we don't expect every art house film to save the rain forest.

Yet we still talk about games as if they're all the same. We talk about how games could reenergize education, without having a nuanced conversation about *which* games and *why*. We worry about the impact of violent games on young people, without necessarily being able to distinguish for ourselves differences among various conflict and weapons-based games in the way we could compare, say, an Arnold Schwarzenegger movie to *A Clockwork Orange* to a Bugs Bunny cartoon.

I believe it's time to up our game in this conversation. Why hasn't this happened before? Part of the blame lies with us game researchers, for being too busy talking among ourselves to share what we've learned in a way that makes sense to people who don't devote all their waking hours to studying games. Part of the blame lies with the medium itself. Great games can take hours to play, and years to master; sometimes you can't appreciate them without a high level of skill. Meanwhile, personal knowledge about games builds up in a random and scattershot way. If you're older than forty, you may not have had much exposure to games growing up. Even if you grew up gaming, you may only know a few genres well. To go back to the film analogy, you'd be missing a big piece of the puzzle in judging film if all you'd ever seen were art films. We don't take game literacy classes in school, so we aren't ever taught tools and frameworks and a vocabulary to help us understand this medium, the way we learn to interpret literature or film or music in high school and beyond.

So why does this matter? If we don't raise our conversational level about games, we run some big risks. One is throwing the new baby out with the bathwater. This almost happened with comic books. Because they started out as a medium for children, critics for many years failed to see them as anything more than sensationalistic kid stuff. Today we have a wide range of brilliant and moving graphic novels, but it took a long time and a lot of struggle to get here.

At this moment there's a Renaissance taking place in games, in the breadth of genres and the range of emotional territory they cover. I'd hate to see this wither on the vine because the cultural conversation never caught up to what was going on. We need to be able to talk about art games and "indie" games the ways we do about art and indie film.

Another risk is placing high hopes on games designed for the public good—as many nonprofits, health organizations, and social enterprises are doing—without realizing that bad game design can undermine the most noble of ambitions. It's quite possible to make terrible, dull, and unappealing games for learning or training or health. We need to have a language for discerning among these games—are they doing their job well or poorly? How can you tell? What makes them good?

In this book, I will share what I know about one aspect of games that I've been researching for many years: how they create emotion. People who aren't on the inside of the game world often tell me they fear that games numb players to other people, stifling empathy and creating a generation of isolated, antisocial loners. In these pages, I argue that the reverse is true: that games can actually play a powerful role in creating empathy and other strong, positive emotional experiences. It makes me sad that this is not common knowledge, but it doesn't surprise me. After all, games reveal these emotionally positive qualities over time, through the act of playing. An observer can't see these qualities by occasionally watching other people play. Yet most people do not have the time to immerse themselves in play and develop enough mastery to fully experience the emotionally transformative aspects of games. What is needed, really, is a guided tour of exactly how games can influence empathy, emotion, and social connection, with examples that unpack the experience of the gamer. That is what you'll find in the chapters ahead. This book also offers useful framing concepts for sorting out what's going on emotionally for players, and for discerning what any given game is doing to provoke emotion and social connection.

In chapter 1, I introduce two qualities that separate games from all other media—choice and flow. I show how game developers build upon these qualities, evoking players' social emotions using avatars, nonplayer characters (NPCs), and character customization in solo play situations. Chapter 2 moves from solo play to social play, demonstrating how avatars and NPCs operate emotionally through three additional design techniques for shaping social play—coordinated action, role-play, and social situations. Chapter 3 shows how designers are using physical movement to enhance the emotional terrain of games, while chapter 4 looks at long-distance connection and networked play. Throughout, I draw on examples ranging from popular "AAA" games to art games and avant-garde projects. My hope is to expose readers to a larger variety of game genres and experiences than they may otherwise encounter, toward expanding broader literacy about games and the unexplored possibilities they offer. I hope this book will enable readers to critically examine games that claim to accomplish emotional goals for players, using the terms and tools for analysis in these pages. I also hope this book will raise the esteem in which games are held as an innovative and powerful medium for doing what all media do—helping us understand ourselves and explore what it means to be human.

1 A Series of Interesting Choices: The Building Blocks of Emotional Design

People talk about how games don't have the emotional impact of movies. I think they do—they just have a different palette. I never felt pride, or guilt, watching a movie.

—Will Wright, designer of *The Sims*[1]

Compelling games don't happen by accident, any more than do gripping novels, movies, or music. In all these media, creators draw from a well-defined set of strategies and techniques to create a specific emotional experience. Musicians, for instance, might use a minor key and slower tempo to create a sad or anxious mood (at least in the West). Film directors use close-ups to create intimacy. Game developers, too, have been honing techniques that lead players through intentionally designed emotional experience, whether that experience is the offbeat and comic mood of *The Sims* or *Angry Birds*, or the dramatic intensity of *Call of Duty*. Unlike film, fiction, or music, there isn't yet a common language among designers, players, and society at large for what is going on and why in the hearts and minds of players. This chapter introduces building block concepts taken from game design and game research, which I believe offer insight into and provide a shared language for how, exactly, games move us. Specifically, two unique qualities, choice and flow, set games apart from other media in terms of potential for emotional impact. Layering techniques for evoking social emotions onto this foundation gives games their unique power to create empathy and connection. This chapter introduces three design innovations—avatars, nonplayer characters, and character customization—that are primary drivers for social emotions in players.

Meaningful Choices

At their heart, games differ from other media in one fundamental way: they offer players the chance to influence outcomes through their own efforts.[2] With rare exception, this is not true of film, novels, or television. Readers and viewers of these other media follow along, reacting to the story and its twists and turns, without having a direct personal impact on the events they witness. In games, players have the unique ability to control what unfolds. As Sid Meier, designer of the best-selling game *Civilization*, once said, "a [good] game is a series of interesting choices."[3]

Actions with consequences—interesting choices—unlock a new set of emotional possibilities for game designers. Ultimately, these possibilities exist because our feelings in everyday life, as well as games, are integrally tied to our goals, our decisions, and their consequences.[4] People go through a rapid and automatic set of evaluations as things happen to them, about what each event might mean for their goals and plans. Emotions arise in the context of these appraisals, and help guide quick and appropriate actions. Psychology researchers focused on this appraisal process, in fact, have used videogames as research instruments, in order to tightly control situations and demonstrate how particular challenges lead to emotional responses. For example, adding events that match up to someone's in-game goals reliably induces more pride and joy in players, while adding events that block their goals leads to anger.[5]

Researchers can actually observe the traces of meaningful choices in the brain activity of gamers. Neuropsychology researchers created an experiment in which some participants played a game and others watched a live video stream of another person playing (essentially like watching a movie). The researchers used fMRI equipment to get a glimpse of everyone's brain activity. The active gamers showed more activation of "reward-related mesolimbic neural circuits"—parts of the brain associated with motivation and reward[6]—than those who watched passively. Interacting with the game shifted the emotional patterns observed in the players' brains, demonstrating how we human beings experience particular rewards and emotions from the act of playing.

To the human brain, playing a game is more like actually running a race than watching a film or reading a short story about a race. When I run, I make a series of choices about actions I will take that might affect whether I win. I feel a sense of mastery or failure depending on whether I successfully execute the actions in the ways I intended. My emotions ebb and flow as I make these choices and see what happens as a result. I feel a sense of consequence and responsibility for my choices. In the end, I am to blame for the outcomes, because they arise from my own actions. This rich set of feelings that I have about the solo experience of running depends on the active role that I play in the experience—that is, on my own meaningful choices. In the chapters ahead, we'll explore how game designers build upon the feelings generated by choice and control to create a broad palette of emotional experiences for players.

Flow

The ability to choose and control your actions gives rise to the second unique quality of games: the ease with which players can enter a pleasurable, optimal performance state that psychology researcher Mihaly Csikzentmihalyi calls "flow." When people are in flow—when musicians play at their best, when athletes are in "the zone," when programmers stay up all night creating brilliant code—time seems to melt away and personal problems disappear. Well-designed games, with the control they offer users over actions in a novel world, readily engage players in a flow state.

When Csikzentmihalyi and his colleagues studied people in flow, they isolated eight factors defining this optimal state— factors that will sound familiar to anyone who finds games compelling.

- a challenging activity requiring skill
- a merging of action and awareness
- clear goals
- direct, immediate feedback
- concentration on the task at hand
- a sense of control
- a loss of self-consciousness
- an altered sense of time

The role of the flow state in games was not lost on Csikzentmihalyi. In his book *Finding Flow*, he calls out games, "developed over the centuries for the express purpose of enriching life with enjoyable experiences,"[7] as excellent producers of flow in human beings.

Game designers such as Jenova Chen, who did his master's thesis work on flow,[8] have found flow theory useful in exploring the deeper "why" behind the fun players have with games. Chen intentionally tried to reproduce the eight major factors of flow in his game design practice. By doing so, he developed some famously engaging games including *Journey* (discussed in chapter 4). Chen believes flow theory provides a working model for game designers, encouraging them to keep players in a sweet spot where they have the right amount of ability to meet the challenges at hand. Too little ability can result in anxiety and frustration; too little challenge can result in boredom or apathy (see figure 1.1).

Increasingly, game designers aim to offer players interesting choices that fall within that sweet spot, generating flow. Flow theory has been a boon to the game design and research communities, moving discussion of what players feel and why away from the vague, if positive, notion of "fun" and into more nuanced emotional territory that can be shaped through design choices. When players discuss the emotions they feel when playing games,[9] much of their vocabulary relates to flow (curiosity, excitement, challenge, elation, or triumph) or the lack thereof (frustration, confusion, discouragement). Thus, flow theory offers a useful lens for understanding the unique emotional power of games compared to other media.

Social Emotions

When designers offer interesting choices and keep players in flow, they're able to also start evoking another class of feelings

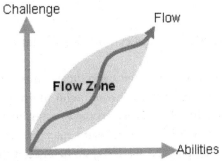

Figure 2 Player in-game flow experience

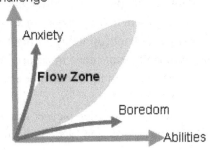

Figure 3 Player encounters psychic entropies

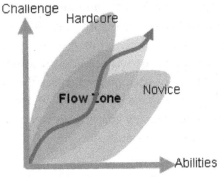

Figure 4 Different players and flow zones

Figure 1.1

Jenova Chen's diagram of the "flow zone."

Source: Jenova Chen, "Flow in Games," MFA thesis, University of Southern California, 2006, http://www.jenovachen.com/flowingames/Flow _in_games_final.pdf

in their players—the rich social emotions we experience in relationship with others. In the 1980s, then fledgling game company Electronic Arts (EA) released an employee recruitment advertisement that asked "Can a Computer Make You Cry?"[10] This phrase became a rallying cry for those in the game industry interested in creating social feelings in players such as affection, camaraderie, empathy, or even grief and sadness.[11]

This was not an unreasonable question for EA to ask, given what was known about other media. Film and novels, for example, can evoke powerful social emotional responses. People read or watch or listen, start to feel immersed in the situation being presented/described, and then feel as if they were there. They begin to care about the characters and situations as if they were real. It is not uncommon, or shameful, to cry over something happening in a film or a book.

It's also true that over time, some viewers/readers form powerful attachments to characters, a phenomenon known as "parasocial interaction."[12] Media creators encourage these strong feelings of connection and cultivate them through strategic design elements. For example, TV hosts may make conversational asides to viewers to generate a feeling of intimacy and familiarity. Likewise, film directors often shoot at close range to create the illusion of intimate distance between the character and the viewer. Such techniques amplify identification with the virtual people and situations.

Experts in an area of psychology called "grounded cognition" argue that these techniques evoke emotion because they mirror the way our brains make sense of the world around us in everyday life. They posit that our brains compare what we sense and experience in any given moment to our past experiences (whether "real" or "mediated"—that is, created by media) in order to come up with a set of emotional and cognitive responses that are "grounded" in experience.[13] So if we see or hear (or form a mental picture of) a person experiencing feelings in a social setting that we, too, are immersed in, our brains are "tricked" into believing that a real social experience is taking place. Of course we engage this delusion willingly—it allows us to experience alternate situations and ways of being human, which in turn informs our own experience of being human.

This tradition, as old as oral storytelling, still provides an effective way to share emotional and social wisdom and experience. Yet in any medium other than games, we are only witnesses, not actors, and cannot affect the outcomes of the stories before us.

Grounded cognition theory helps explain what it is about games that changes the range of emotional experiences possible for players when they take on an alternate identity or social situation during play. Consider this example that led to the chapter's epigraph from Will Wright, designer of the best-selling PC game franchise of all time, *The Sims*. Wright describes the first time he played *Black and White: Creature Isle*.[14] In this game, the player has a creature that he trains, who acts as his go-between with the villagers in the game world. The player can mold an evil creature by treating it badly, or create a moral creature by treating it kindly. Curious about the outcome of ill treatment, Wright began to slap his creature—then was astonished to find himself feeling guilty about it, even though this was very obviously not a real being with real emotions. This capacity to evoke actual feelings of guilt from a fictional experience is unique to games. A reader or filmgoer may feel many emotions when presented with horrific fictional acts on the page or screen, but responsibility and guilt are generally not among them. At most, they may feel a sense of uneasy collusion. Conversely, a film viewer might feel joyful when the protagonist wins, but is not likely to feel a sense of personal responsibility and pride. Because they depend on active player choice, games have an additional palette of social emotions at their disposal.

Brenda Brathwaite Romero's *Train* (see figure 1.2) offers an elegant example of a game that calls on interesting choices and the flow state to implicate players in social choices and outcomes. Winner of the Vanguard Award at IndieCade (the primary venue for showcasing independent games in the United States), this tabletop board game is part of Romero's Mechanics

Figure 1.2
Brenda Brathwaite Romero's *Train*.
Source: Train (exhibited only, 2009); photo courtesy of Brenda Romero

Is the Message series. (A game *mechanic* is an action that a player can take that changes the game state.[15]) She created these games specifically to evoke a feeling difficult to achieve in other media—complicity.[16] Players of *Train* move boxcars full of passengers from one place to another, dealing with obstacles and challenges along the way. Only at the end of the game do they learn the train's destination: Auschwitz. Some players realize what's happening midgame and turn their attention to saving as many passengers as they can. Almost all players feel strong emotions after they have experienced the endgame, whether or not they realized what was going on in the midst of play. Romero says: "Ultimately, I think the power of a game lies in its ability to bring us close to the subject. There is no other medium that has this power. I saw people cry over *Train*, not just once, but multiple times. People watching, playing, those trying to save the passengers. That's powerful, and it's the medium that does that."[17]

In *Train*, Romero creates a tension by juxtaposing the satisfying, flow-style emotions the player feels while mastering the system and rules of the game with the negative emotions that arise from the social context of these actions. In this regard, *Train* can be seen as a meditation on similar painful and horrific emotional juxtapositions that may have occurred in the actual historical situation.

Romero's other board games in the Mechanics Is the Message series are equally stark and simple, encouraging a focus on the systems and rules of games that works to forge complicity. They bring home the power of games, whether digital or not, to evoke deep, socially based emotions triggered by choice and consequence.

Avatars—Inhabitable Protagonists

Since the days of ancient Greek theater[18] and probably far earlier, storytellers have created specific characters with whom viewers or readers could identify, whose eyes provided the primary point of view—protagonists. Game designers have adopted and adapted this technique for grounding a player's identification with in-game events. In gaming, the protagonist is known as "the player character" or "avatar." As with protagonists in film, the player learns about avatars through how they look and how they react to other characters (in games, there can be software-driven nonplayer characters that a player meets and interacts with as if they are real other people in the game's story world). However, the avatar's personal qualities and capacities are also reflected in what it is possible for the player to *do* on multiple psychological levels (see figure 1.3). The player moves through the game world taking actions as this person, adopting his or her concerns and struggling toward his or her goals. Players controlling avatars project themselves into the character on four levels: visceral, cognitive, social, and fantasy. The player's prosthetic body, with its specific capabilities and tendencies, becomes a vehicle for action. The player builds skill and strength over time, which is reflected in this virtual body in the game world (this is the "visceral level" of character experience). Certain strategies, actions, and reactions are rewarded over others, through designer choices about game mechanics and outcomes (this is the "cognitive level" of experience). Inhabiting the avatar's social persona allows the player to try out social qualities they may not normally possess (providing a "social level" of experience). All of these design choices work together to allow the

Figure 1.3
Players project themselves more deeply onto game avatars than protagonists in other media because avatars offer action possibilities at multiple psychological levels.
Source: Katherine Isbister, *Better Game Characters by Design: A Psychological Approach* (Boca Raton, FL: CRC/Morgan Kaufmann, 2006); image courtesy of CRC Press, Taylor & Francis Group

player to explore alternate fantasy selves through actual in-game performance (providing a "fantasy level" of experience). Over the course of gameplay, players extend themselves further into the motivations and the visceral, cognitive, social, and fantasy possibilities of the avatar, forging an identification grounded in observation as well as action and experience.[19]

Consider, for example, a snowboarding game. The player viscerally feels like the snowboarding avatar. Through her controller, she may have a physical sensation of bouncing along on virtual snow. She hears the sounds of her board sliding, the thwack of the board landing after she makes a jump. If the game is in the third-person perspective (where you see your avatar move through the action, as if through a camera hovering above and behind), then the player also sees the avatar make that perfect landing or stutter a bit and recover. On a cognitive level of identification, the player thinks through her choices, deciding which runs to go down and which moves to make, given the strengths and possibilities of her avatar. She can ham it up for the virtual crowd in the game as if she is the snowboarder (social identification). All of this allows her to enjoy performing and experiencing the fantasy identity of a champion snowboarder, winning races and conquering mountains.

This joining of player to virtual self through avatar-based action marks a core innovation that games have brought to media, and an extremely powerful one for evoking emotion. Let's look at an example that does some of the same emotional work as *Train*, but in a digital setting, with the added power of a player avatar.

Waco Resurrection is a fascinating and disturbing game that takes as its subject the 1993 Waco siege, in which the government sent agents into the Branch Davidian cult/religious group's compound in Texas. The game's designers at c-level, a Los Angeles-based artist workspace and collective, developed the game specifically for art gallery–style settings. Inhabiting an avatar of cult leader David Koresh, the player must defend the Branch Davidian compound against government agents. The game engine (a software framework) used to generate *Waco Resurrection* was originally designed for producing "shooter" games. Thus the look and feel of the game, and the types of player actions it supports, resemble other shooter-style games that players might have encountered in the past. Players can engage in typical shooter mechanics, like firing weapons and killing other characters while moving through indoor and outdoor terrain. The player also has to navigate around other Branch Davidian members in the compound.

The audio soundscape enhances the player's visceral immersion in the experience: at different points, the player hears FBI negotiators, battle sounds, even the voice of God. The artists included audio recordings that FBI agents played to disorient the actual compound members when they launched their assault (i.e., the sounds of drills, screaming animals, etc.).

Waco Resurrection uses a "third-person" perspective for the avatar (see figure 1.4a). Many shooter avatars are portrayed in a "first-person" view, which means the player moves through the game seeing everything as if through that avatar's eyes, including seeing the avatar's hands carrying and shooting weapons as if they are in the player's peripheral vision. There is ongoing debate in the game design community as to whether and when to use a first- versus third-person view for the avatar in a game. Some players report that a first-person perspective helps them immerse themselves completely in their alternate identity; some observers feel first-person shooter games are more likely to incite

Figure 1.4a, b

In *Waco Resurrection*, the player inhabits the role of cult leader David Koresh. In gallery installations of the game, players wore David Koresh helmet-masks that had embedded speakers and microphones (Eddo Stern, *Waco Resurrection 2003–2004*, web video, 2:49, http://www.eddostern.com/video/wacobroadbandlow.mov).

Source: *Waco Resurrection* (c-level, 2004); image courtesy of Eddo Stern

real violence.[20] In *Waco Resurrection*, the third-person perspective helps continually remind players who they are supposed to be in the game.

The game's designers heighten the connection between player and avatar by requiring players to wear custom helmets designed for the experience (see figure 1.4b). On the outside, these look like a low-polygon (less rich and precise) version of David Koresh's head and face. In a gallery setting, these helmets also serve the purpose of cutting off spectators from the actual identity of the player, whose head disappears into a creepy blurred version of Koresh. A microphone inside the helmet allows the player to speak key phrases aloud to use special powers in the game. For example, saying "wrath of god" brings a rainfall of flaming bibles down from the sky, killing everyone around the player. Saying "gun show" brings up a circle of AK-47s around the player that can be used to fire at everything around him. The spoken commands bring the player into an even more direct and intimate connection with the avatar's choices and (imagined) mindset.

Eddo Stern, one of the creators, had this to say about the power of the game:

One of the differences in making a game about an historical event is the nature of identification and implication. Games require the users to act and as such appear to implicate the player in the actions of the avatar they are controlling. This is rather obvious but does create new emotional experiences. Imagine a documentary about Hitler vs. a fictional film with an actor playing as Hitler vs. a game where the player plays as Hitler. The most common criticisms we heard about *Waco* were that the game is in bad taste, that the game is exploitative, that the game was pro Davidian/pro Koresh. The bad taste and exploitation criticism stem from people struggling to consider that games can be made about serious issues while still providing some ambiguity. The second criticism of the game being politically skewed assumes that Koresh as a protagonist = a

Hero in the game—a unique issue that games reveal as a film about Hitler would likely not draw this criticism or a film about David Koresh.[21]

Inhabiting the persona of the cult figurehead at the heart of the episode is a unique way to experience the "extreme psychosocial phenomenon" of the historical event. The game's designers see Koresh as "a paradoxical embodiment of the current [2004] political landscape—he is both the besieged religious other and the logical extension of the neo-conservative millennial vision." They see *Waco* as a "primal scene of American fear: the apocalyptic visionary—an American tradition stretching back to Jonathan Edwards—confronts the heathen 'other.'"[22]

Waco Resurrection received an honorary mention at Ars Electronica, one of the most prestigious venues for media art. The artists broke ground in exploiting digital games' capacity to evoke agency and blur identity, producing a work that transcends simple stereotypes and that leaves the player uneasy, with a rich and unresolved emotional response. *Waco* exposes the potential of games to reopen problematic cultural episodes or issues for visceral reexploration, toward deeper understanding and continuing conversation. The game makes powerful use of the avatar to put the player (and spectators) into dialogue with the work and with the historical events it seeks to portray.

Through an original and potentially disturbing use of avatars, *Waco Resurrection* brings players into the mind of an infamous renegade; at the opposite end of the spectrum, *Cart Life* gets players to inhabit the emotional headspace of more mundane everyday urban types who might otherwise go completely unnoticed. Designed as a "retail simulator for windows," according to developer Richard Hofmeier,[23] the game swept three of the Independent Games Festival awards at the 2013 Game Developers

Conference in San Francisco, including the Excellence in Narrative award. As one game journalist describes it:

A young mom trying to provide for her daughter. A Ukrainian immigrant hoping to make a new life. A well-traveled bagel chef who can't bring himself to walk away from the white-knuckle intensity of the food service industry. The heroes of *Cart Life* are anything but your typical video game protagonists. They are ordinary people, doing their best to get by in a world that doesn't make it easy. By putting you in the shoes of these three individuals and letting you share in their struggles, *Cart Life* becomes a moving ode to the trials and tribulations of regular people who work themselves to the bone day in and day out just to get by.[24]

The player chooses one of three cart vendors to play, and then must engage in the work of running the cart, by commuting to and from work, managing inventory, chatting with customers, and the like (see figure 1.5a–d). Each of the vendors must also navigate personal challenges. For example, Melanie, who runs a coffee cart, needs money to help in her custody struggles and has to pick up her daughter, Laura, every day from school. The player, who gets to know Laura through walks and at home, works to balance Melanie's goals through her everyday decisions.

Hofmeier emphasizes his attempt at generating a realistic experience: "I wanted to make as realistic a game as I could. Sometimes I hear about how the larger game-playing audience is maturing, but I don't buy it. I wanted a game like this when I was a kid—I wanted to learn how to live." He interviewed street vendors about their lives to make sure he got the details right.[25] Notably he did not go after this emotional realism with high-resolution graphics—the art style of the game is grayscale and pixelated, and the music has a "chip tunes" aesthetic (a tinny, synthesized sound, like music from older game consoles that lacked sophisticated stereo output).

b

c

d

Figure 1.5a–d
Cart Life: (a) overview, (b) introduction of Vinny (one of three player character choices), (c) buying supplies, and (d) preparing bagels.
Source: Cart Life (freeware, 2011); image courtesy of Richard Hofmeier

Cart Life masterfully evokes in players the feeling that there is never enough time, while also providing sweet moments with the customers and relatives and friends in the vendors' everyday lives. Unlike many mainstream commercial games that cast the player in a heroic, larger-than-life persona, *Cart Life* puts the player deeply into an ordinary-scale human life, and still succeeds in creating feelings of struggle and triumph and connection. The aesthetic techniques and human subject matter of *Cart*

Life help illuminate the broader emotional terrain that today's independent games offer to players, in part through the use of astute avatar and nonplayer character choices.

Nonplayer Characters—"Living, Breathing" Others in the Game World

Solitary gameplay is not by definition lonely. In fact, digital games frequently include virtual "living, breathing" others who provide support, resistance, and local color. Game designers use dynamic and reactive engagement with these other characters who populate a game's story world to add to the emotional palette of games as a medium. In a film, the viewer learns about the protagonist through his or her interactions with other people in the narrative world of the film. In a game, players can themselves interact with those others—spending hours journeying alongside them, struggling to rescue them, sometimes experiencing betrayal by them and losing hard-won ground as a result. In a game, a nonplayer character can make a joke that lightens the mood during a slog, provide assistance in the nick of time, even sacrifice himself so that the player can carry on and win the day. This dynamic engagement with a virtual other lies at the root of feelings such as Wright's guilt for slapping his creature. Interactions with NPCs move players beyond "para-social" feelings into consequential social experiences with accompanying social emotions and behaviors.

My own dissertation research at Stanford University helps demonstrate the power of interactive engagement with NPCs.[26] I was investigating whether an NPC's dominant or submissive style "personality" would affect how persuasive that NPC was in a team situation. Participants in my research worked on a task called the desert survival problem. They were told to imagine that they had crashed in the desert in a small plane. When they came to, items from the plane were scattered around them—things like a compress kit, a book, a raincoat. They had to rank the items in order of survival importance. Then, each person had a "conversation" with a very simple NPC that would try to convince them to change their rankings of a few items (see figure 1.6).

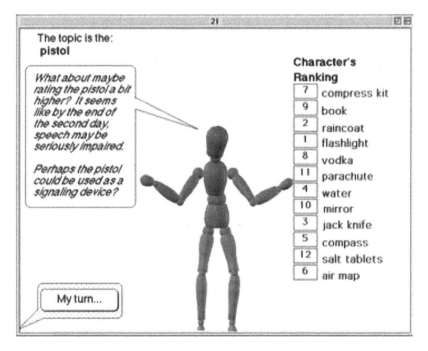

Figure 1.6
The NPC in my dissertation research making suggestions about changing rankings of items in the desert survival task.
Source: Katherine Isbister, "Reading Personality in Onscreen Interactive Characters: An Examination of Social Psychological Principles of Consistency, Personality Match, and Situational Attribution Applied to Interaction with Characters," Ph.D. dissertation, Stanford University, 1998

The NPCs showed signs of submissiveness or dominance in their body postures and in the way they phrased their advice. For example, in figure 1.6, the NPC has taken a dominant stance (arms wide) but is using hesitant, submissive-style language ("what about maybe" and "perhaps"). In the study, each person saw one of four versions of the NPC—consistent dominant cues, consistent submissive cues, or mixed (dominant body with submissive phrasing, or submissive body with dominant phrasing). As would be the case with real human beings, those who interacted with the mixed-signals NPCs were less influenced. They made fewer changes to their own ranking of the items than participants in the study who saw consistent NPCs. In real life, consistency in nonverbal cues is associated with honesty and trustworthiness. It is amazing that these sorts of responses hold true for engaging with virtual humans as well.[27] To the extent that NPCs display humanlike actions and reactions, we engage them using social norms and intuitive emotional responses. This means that game designers can create powerful feelings in players when they make use of relationships that players form with NPCs.

In 2008, a student (Corey Nolan) and I surveyed a range of players on what moments in games had actually made them cry (in a sort of answer to EA's advertisement). The most frequently cited moments involved the death of NPCs with whom players had spent considerable time during gameplay. Players wept over losing valued and trustworthy companions.[28] The number one example from our survey was from 1983—an entirely text-based, interactive fiction adventure game named *Planetfall*. In this game, the player spends a lot of time with an NPC robot named Floyd. As *Creative Computing* magazine put it in a review of the game, "the most imaginative and cleverly written part of the entire game, Floyd, besides being hysterically funny through most of the adventure, evokes in the player of *Planetfall* authentic feelings of affection and attachment."[29] In her famous academic treatise on games, *Hamlet on the Holodeck*, Janet Murray points out: "The memory of Floyd the Robot's noble self-sacrifice remains with players even years later as something directly experienced. 'He sacrificed himself for me,' is the way one twenty-year-old former player described it to me."[30]

Accomplished game designers use a range of subtle social cues from NPCs to produce feelings in players, putting NPCs into powerful and consequent social relationships with the player/avatar. In the game *Hush*, for example, game designers Jamie Antonisse and Devon Johnson made use of one of the most powerful human relationships—mother and child—and one of the most emotionally irresistible sounds—a baby crying—to create a simple, vignette-style game that is powerfully evocative (see figure 1.7). Created for a course the designers took while completing an MFA program at USC, Hush has the player control a Rwandan Tutsi mother, Liliane. She must "sing" a lullaby to her child to keep the child quiet, or risk the attention of Hutu soldiers who may kill them both. The player must press a letter key as that letter appears on-screen. The letters slowly appear, brighten, then fade. Hitting the key at just the right moment keeps things quiet. If the player fails too many times, the baby's crying increases in intensity, the player sees silhouettes of soldiers, and the encounter ends with the mother's gasp, gunfire, and the screen fading to red, indicating that the mother and child have been discovered. Despite (or perhaps because of) the spare, simple artwork, the player becomes caught up in the responsibility of taking care of the child, and filled with dread about what may happen if he does not succeed.

Figure 1.7
In *Hush*, the player must soothe a baby to keep it quiet and safe from soldiers outside.
Source: Hush (freeware, 2008); image courtesy of Jamie Antonisse and Devon Johnson

Playing the game and caring for the virtual child create a form of participation and involvement, and dramatically personalize the struggles of Rwandans. Choosing a universally understood, archetypal role (mother) for the player, an NPC that the player is physiologically hardwired to react to (baby), and a familiar activity (singing a lullaby) all contribute to the ease of immersion and identification that the game provides. To play it is to become, during gameplay, emotionally involved in the personal fears and consequences of this conflict. It is what Bogost, Ferrari, and Schweizer[31] would term an "editorial game"—a game designed to persuade the player in some way (in this case, to activate the player to notice and care about the human costs of a real-world struggle happening far away). Advocates of "games for change"—games designed to impact a player's actions and growth toward advancing some kind of social good—believe this sort of immersion by enactment and identification may be an important tool in reaching younger audiences who are turning less and less to traditional information sources such as television and print journalism.

The game *Love Plus* uses NPCs to create another emotionally charged social interaction—courtship. In dating sims like *Love Plus* (a genre popular in Japan, though less popular in the United States so far), the player works to woo over an NPC (usually female) so that she and the player are "dating." The end result might be a light romance, true love, or maybe even sim sex, depending upon the game subgenre (variations on dating games range from chaste to pornographic). Players try to improve their in-game personal qualities in order to attract their chosen one; meanwhile, they must choose the right things to say and do to court her and keep her love once she has admitted that she cares. Some dating sims are tethered to real time; many offer ways around this with the ability to preschedule actions and playing times. Some explore alternate input strategies such as voice and touch screens.

At the start of *Love Plus*, which is set in a high school, you can choose one of three girls to pursue: Nene, Manaka, and Rinko (figure 1.8). You meet Nene, a sort of older sister type, at your part-time job at a restaurant and Manaka, a wealthy, sporty girl a year ahead of you in school, at a tennis club. Rinko, your third option, is younger and shier than the other two, and is a bit

Figure 1.8
Love Plus, a Japanese dating sim released on the Nintendo DS platform, has three female characters with whom the player can attempt to forge a relationship.
Source: Love Plus 3DS (Otaku Gaming/Konami, 2009)

standoffish when you meet on a library committee. (As a player, you don't have a preset name: you're referred to in the first person, but you can add nicknames the girls might use once they feel closer to you.)

The game has two phases. In the first, you decide which of these three girls to pursue, and set about courting her (figure 1.9a, b and 1.9c). In the second, once you've won her over, you try to maintain a good relationship. During the courting phase, you have a hundred days to win her over; each day, you can choose four actions. Some build your personal characteristics (health, knowledge, sensibility, and charm), and some create openings for you to interact with the three girls. Over the course of your courtship, you receive progressively richer methods of communication with the object of your affections—for example, she shares her mobile number so you can text, and she'll walk to and from school with you. As one reviewer describes it:

How the girl gets closer to you is quite interesting. At first, I see Nene at school and I'm the one calling out for her to chat. As time passes, she will be the one to approach you instead. Early on, I was the one offering to walk together with her after school, but later on she will be the one taking the initiative. Also, there were no morning events until the 40th day I think, when she started meeting me walking towards school. This is where *Love Plus* seemed impressive. Each of these events has some unique dialogue. Yes, even the repeating mundane events like walking to and from school, as well as idle chats at school and also in the evening. She always had something else to say.[32]

Once your sweetheart confesses she likes you, the game moves into a second phase, where you must retain her affection. You can read about local events, news, and hot spots for dates through an

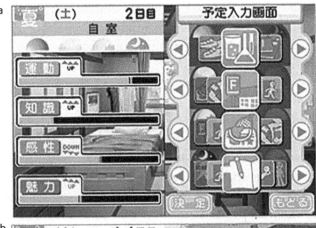

Figure 1.9a, b

The courting phase of *Love Plus*, in which the player chooses daily actions toward successfully wooing a particular girl.

Source: Love Plus 3DS (Otaku Gaming/Konami, 2009); bluemist, "Love Plus: Impressions," *bluemist*, September 5, 2009, http://bluemist .animeblogger.net/archives/love-plus-1/; image courtesy of bluemist anime blog

c

Figure 1.9c
Scenes of a player's courtship with Nene.
Source: Love Plus 3DS (Otaku Gaming/Konami, 2009); bluemist, "Love Plus:
Impressions," *bluemist*, September 5, 2009, http://bluemist.animeblogger
.net/archives/love-plus-1/; image courtesy of bluemist anime blog

d

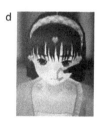

Figure 1.9d
Kissing is simulated in *Love Plus* with stylus caresses to the character.
Source: Love Plus 3DS (Otaku Gaming/Konami, 2009); bluemist, "Love
Plus: Impressions," *bluemist*, September 5, 2009, http://bluemist
.animeblogger.net/archives/love-plus-1/; image courtesy of bluemist
anime blog

in-game Internet connection, or find clubs and restaurants on a map. As described by the same player:

This phase adds more gameplay. Aside from the text messaging system, you can also "call" your girlfriend, either if you want to meet for a little chat and "cuddling" . . . or to schedule/cancel a "date" (a more eventful form of chats and cuddling). . . . Me and Nene have been to the karaoke bar twice. While there are some repeating conversations in each, there have been unique ones which surprised me. I didn't hear her sing at the first one, but she "sang" a bit at the second outing. Whoa.[33]

Love Plus was designed for play on the Nintendo DS, which has a touch screen and stylus, as well as a built-in microphone. These let you speak to your friend in some limited fashion, and even "kiss" using a curious motion of the stylus (see figure 1.9d). When kissed, the character acts giggly, modest, and cute.[34]

Love Plus simulates the circumstances and details of falling in love, of getting to know someone and charming them, and of seeing affection blossom in response. Scenes play out in school hallways, at tennis courts, and at other mundane locations in which teen love flourishes. Perhaps a good analogue in American media culture would be romance novels, which allow readers to experience a para-social romance—to be a silent, over-the-shoulder observer of two characters coming together. But in this case, the player gets to take part in this process, thanks to the game's artful use of NPCs and the human brain's experience of intimacy as it emerges from the small actions and reactions of everyday interaction between sweethearts.

This experience can feel so real, in fact, that some players seem to prefer it to flesh-and-blood romance. In 2009, a *Love Plus* player went to Guam and officially married Nene, one of the three girls in the game.[35] This player, who dubbed himself "Sal 9000," seemed quite aware of the absurdity of the choice,

Figure 1.10
Sal 9000 with Nene, a character from *Love Plus*. They were married in Guam in 2009.
Source: Know Your Meme/Boing Boing video, 2009, https://www.youtube.com/watch?v=hsikPswAYUM

but also enamored with the idea of blurring real and virtual identity and affection (see figure 1.10). The makers of *Love Plus* have intentionally capitalized upon this blurring of boundaries to promote their game. In 2010 they partnered with beachside resort town Atami, featured in the game, offering hotel specials "for two," and photo opportunities with a life-size model of each of the game's characters.[36]

Journalists have made much of the rise of the "2-D lover" culture in Japan—(mostly) men who choose to bond with and claim relationships with imaginary women.[37] In a *New York Times* article,[38] the author draws a connection between the rise of affection for digital characters and the collapse of traditional romance and connection—she points out that 50 percent of men and women in Japan said they were "not going out with anybody," and that more than a quarter of single people ages 30–34 claimed to be virgins. Some advocates of 2-D love see it as a rejection of the materialism and emptiness of modern romance in favor of an almost Zen-like acceptance of desire as an illusion in itself. Others point out that they would simply not succeed in attracting a "real" woman, and that this alternative allows them to experience strong feelings and a sustaining bond without fear of rejection. As one player put it, "It's hard to explain in words, but it's a feeling similar to romance. Sasami gave me the will to keep going."[39]

Unlike a real-life suitor, a *Love Plus* player can feel pretty confident that he will in the end be "loved," if only he takes the time to master the nuances of engagement preferred by the NPC of his choice. The game world offers a sort of rigorous and comforting fairness to romance. Unfortunately, such a world requires a significant time investment in a romance that can never provide the connection, companionship, and interdependence of a relationship with another human being. These characters cannot truly reciprocate, but can only hold a mirror up to us and to our longings. However we might feel about players choosing virtual over actual love, the game showcases the startling power of NPCs for evoking intimacy and a disconcertingly real sense of connection for players.

Character Customization

Another way game designers encourage emotional identification and connection with avatars and NPCs is by allowing players control over how these characters look and act. Probably the most famous example of in-depth character customization possibilities provided to players is *The Sims*. Launched in 2000, with four major new releases and many expansion packs added since, the game has been described as a "living dollhouse." Players choose and customize multiple semiautonomous characters or Sims (see figure 1.11), create a home for them, and then oversee their lives (see figure 1.12). The player must help the Sims meet

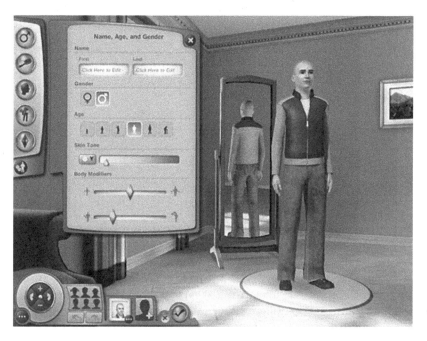

Figure 1.11
Character creation system from *The Sims 3*. Players can choose the character's name, gender, age, weight, facial features, coloring, clothing, voice qualities, some key traits (such as light sleeper, dislikes children, schmoozer, or slob), a few favorite items, and a lifetime wish (such as becoming a chess legend or a superstar athlete).
Source: The Sims 3 (Electronic Arts, 2009); image taken from Wikipedia

Figure 1.12
Screenshot from the original *The Sims* game. The player queues up actions for the Sim (at top left) by pointing and clicking on objects in the environment and on the Sim, making sure that the basic needs of the character are met. Here, the Sim is about to go and play the piano.
Source: The Sims (Electronic Arts, 2000); image taken from Will Wright Fansite, http://www.will-wright.com/willshistory12.php

their basic needs (food, rest, companionship, a home, money, and some fun) and support them as they chase their dreams. Players can use money earned by the Sims to purchase clothing, furniture, and other lifestyle accessories. The Sims' internal parameters (some of which can be tweaked by the player) give them preferences for certain living conditions and other Sims; they can get out of sorts and unhappy if the player doesn't handle things well. They can even die if neglected (through house fires, starvation, lack of sleep, and the like).

The main delight of playing with the Sims is watching them go about their virtual lives, both with and without the player's input. As one reviewer puts it:

At first, the fully polygonal characters might look no better than the scenery. But if you leave them alone for even a few minutes, your Sims will do all sorts of things; they'll dance to the radio's music, hunker down in front of the TV, or strike up a conversation. And when your Sims start doing anything, they'll do so with expressive animation that lends them a great deal of personality. When the music is playing, Sims dance the Charleston together; TV-watching Sims will lean forward and gaze intently at the screen or laugh out loud; and conversing Sims will gesticulate appropriately as they chat, dish out insults, tell jokes, and more.[40]

When Sims are "chatting," they are not actually using words. Instead, they are mumbling in a sort of singsong way that cannot be comprehended, but that is nonetheless very expressive. As the reviewer notes: "You can't make out exactly what they're saying, but you can easily infer their intentions from the tone of their voices. Sims will speak, then pause and clear their throats while they're thinking of what to say next, yelp in pain when they cut themselves preparing a meal, or tell naughty limericks as jokes."

Astute character design choices made for *The Sims* series help make the game extremely absorbing. The nonsense babble, and the simplified, cartoony graphics and animations leave more to the player's imagination than if the game had highly polished and detailed dialogue, surfaces, and performances. As Scott McCloud points out in his book *Understanding Comics*,[41] a more abstract and stylized rendition of a character allows viewers to project more of themselves onto the characters, without getting distracted by specific personal qualities and mannerisms.

The game's character customization tools (figure 1.11) allow players to create rough facsimiles of themselves and others they know, providing additional impetus to identify and project. It's quite common to make a Sim of oneself during the course of playing the game. A student of mine and her boyfriend created Sims of themselves and played house in the game world. They found themselves occasionally speaking Simlish to one another in everyday life, echoing their game-world counterparts.

As characters, Sims lie somewhere between avatars and NPCs. Because they have autonomous behaviors, the Sims may surprise their creators with their actions. As designer Wright once remarked, players tend to shift to the third person when this happens—for instance, from "I'm going to do this next" to "Why did he do that?!" This ease of switching from first to third person may be enhanced by the players' visual perspective, from above the action (see figures 1.12 and 1.13).

The animated reactions of Sims (and the emotional tones in their babble) lean toward the broadly comical. For example, a brawl between characters in the game is rendered as a dirt cloud[42] complete with noises and punches. In general, *The Sims* looks and feels like a television sitcom set in a relatively affluent suburb. The Sims live in posh houses and neighborhoods, shop

Figure 1.13
Characters from *The Sims* trapped by a player for several Sim days until they "died."
Source: RanDumbVidz, *Sim's 3 TORTURE!!!!!!!!!!!!!!!!!!*, YouTube video, 1:52, July 6, 2009, http://www.youtube.com/watch?v=7ocOmA0hpqA

for upscale goods, and work jobs and overcome challenges resonant with the upper middle class. The popular expansion packs mirror consumer culture, offering pets, high-end lofts, and "fast lane" accessories. This atmosphere has a way of making light of everything that occurs, even death. Perhaps because the Sims often comically overact, it can feel inconsequential and even entertaining to experiment with Sim fates. Many players have delightedly and publicly recounted the fiendishly creative ways in which they sent Sims to their untimely demise (see figure 1.13). In the case of *The Sims*, power over the characters' lives can feel more like running an ant farm than like making high-stakes decisions for fellow beings.

Some players, however, have inserted their own elements of gritty realism and pathos into the game experience, using customization tools provided by the game company, as well as extending these tools with their own creative hacks. They have created trailer parks (see figure 1.14), pornographic Sims, and

Figure 1.14
A trailer park crafted by *Sims 3* players, and uploaded for others to use as well.
Source: Sims3Addicted, "The Trailer Park," *Mod The Sims*, August 31, 2009, http://www.modthesims.info/download.php?t=367387

Sims in wheelchairs. Some modifications to the game mechanics eliminate the more antisocial comic behavior, such as heckling young children. However these hacks cannot completely alter the overall goofy, slapstick style of the characters' social engagement with one another, such as the dirt-cloud fights or humorous seduction scenes with dramatic tango-style kisses. For the most part, players cannot customize how characters interact with one another, but instead choose their look and their individual desires.

Players interested in telling radically different sorts of stories have made use of *The Sims* as a tool for generating their own graphic novels and movies, by editing video recordings of gameplay and sharing them on fan websites. These stories do explore emotionally fraught social situations—bullying, weddings, breakups, and even eating disorders (see figure 1.15a, b). One player created an ongoing blog narrative about father and daughter Sims who were homeless.[43] This player portrayed homelessness by using the game's mechanics. She designated park benches as the characters' homes and kept as much as possible to the actual in-game interactions that emerged between these characters and others in their neighborhood. Readers of this blog have commented that the story can be painful to follow at times, but also irresistible and emotionally compelling.

These forays by devoted players suggest that while they enjoy the lighthearted comedy and fantasy framing of *The Sims*, they are also interested in exploring other feelings given the real-time simulation of everyday living and interacting that the game provides them. *The Sims* shows the power of character customization both within and beyond the designers' frame of control.

a

I sat there at the table, thinking about what Catherine Gorgas said to me. "You're so fat, Chloe. In fact, Chloe, you're so fat I can't even think how I can even look at you," she told me at school. She bullies everyone, but...I just can't help thinking about what she said.

b

I looked at my waffles. My dad is an exellent chef but I just couldn't eat them. I gripped the fork so tight my hand turned white. I was hungry. But I couldn't eat if I wanted to lose weight.

Figure 1.15a, b
Story created by prettyone27 and posted to *Sims 3* online site, titled "The Beginning: I'm Anorexic"
Source: prettyone27, "The Beginning: I'm Anorexic," *The Sims 3 Community,* July 4, 2010, http://www.thesims3.com/contentDetail.html?contentId=231419

Wrapping Up

In this chapter, I introduced some basic building blocks for evoking player emotion through game design choices. At the root of the emotional power of games lies the fact that games are comprised of choices with consequences. This means the study of game emotions can look more like studying peak performance than media effects, which explains the use of flow theory in game effects research. Because players make their own choices and experience their consequences, game designers have unique powers to evoke emotions—such as guilt and pride—that typically cannot be accessed with other media. Game designers have developed powerful tools for enhancing social emotions that arise from gameplay. Leveraging our innate tendency to respond to social cues as if they were real, designers give players avatars through which to experience the game, and nonplayer characters with whom to interact in emotionally meaningful ways. Designers also offer customization options to players to encourage their projection and emotional attachment to the game and its events. Examples in this chapter have shown how these tools enable exploration of feelings like complicity, and allow designers and players to recreate a range of human situations from running a food cart to taking part in history to falling in love.

Avatars and NPCs allow players to identify and engage in new ways, awakening different kinds of emotions that designers use not just for entertainment, but also for encouraging the deep awareness that travels alongside agency—a feeling of responsibility and of the complexity of relating to other beings. They offer us, as humans, a new bag of tricks for walking in another's shoes and reliving a situation in the present tense. Game designers can viscerally explore cultural issues (e.g., *Waco Resurrection*), inspire activism (e.g., *Hush*), or help players deeply experience an emotional and social scenario that intrigues them (*Love Plus, Cart Life, The Sims*). I believe game designers are really only beginning to explore how to use these capacities to create rich emotional experiences.

Avatars and NPCs also allow, enable, and encourage us to forge deep and meaningful pseudo relationships, raising questions about the role of media in our everyday lives. What purpose might these relationships serve for us? How do they point out issues we face in our everyday interaction with others? How can they make us aware of painful truths and also of wonderful things about being human?

This chapter focused on the design of emotional experiences for solo players. The next chapter adds other players to the mix, exploring what happens for gamers when they play with other people, and how designers make use of these factors in evoking emotions.

2 Social Play: Designing for Multiplayer Emotions

Why Playing *Together* Matters

The isolated gamer sits alone, face illuminated by the blue glow of the screen, lost in a solitary trance. It's a familiar image from movies, TV, and popular culture in general. But the stereotype of the pasty-faced, antisocial game addict belies what we actually know about gamers. In fact, the majority of people who play digital games play them with others.[1] This shouldn't be surprising: from playground tag to chess, card games, and board games to *Minecraft* and *Call of Duty*, the long history of games is primarily a story of rules and equipment created to engage people together socially.[2] When we humans play (aside from the occasional game of solitaire), we usually play together. So before we can grasp the emotional impact of digital games, we need to understand what happens in social games more broadly.

What's different emotionally about social play compared to, say, solitaire?

We know social interaction in general is deeply consequential to human flourishing. Without it, we wither and become despondent, even physically ill.[3] Social play, then, helps address one of the most fundamental of human needs, in ways that solo play (even with charismatic NPCs) probably doesn't. Game researchers have found that emotional responses change when players compete against real people rather than computers. In one experiment, Canadian researchers Mandryk and Inkpen[4] invited experienced digital gamers to bring a friend to their lab, where both played a digital hockey game. Each person played in two different situations—against the computer, and against his or her friend. Using both questionnaires and physiological measures (galvanic skin response [GSR] and muscle activity measured using electromyography [EMG]), the researchers tried to identify differences in how the players experienced each condition. Not surprisingly, they found that people preferred social play. Both the questionnaires (which measured the players' conscious perceptions and preferences) and the physiological measures (which might have differed from the players' self-reported experience) consistently found that playing with a friend led to higher ratings of engagement than playing against the computer. Further, while players reported more boredom when they lost against the computer than when they won, they were equally engaged when playing a friend, whether they were winning or losing. These results corroborate findings from studying the shared experience of other media as well (e.g., social television watching[5]). The upshot: it's more fun to play together than alone.

In chapter 1, we looked at how meaningful choices make gameplay different than experiences of film, television, and novels. Playing together brings meaningful choices into the social interactions of gameplay. To be sure, people socialize during other mediated experiences—laughing and chatting over a TV show or movie. But gameplay is different. When playing together, you and your fellow players take in-game actions that have real consequences for one another's moment-to-moment experience, as well as consequences for one another's in-game virtual bodies and selves. Thus games provide us with opportunities for both sociability *and* social play.[6] To go back to the snowboarding game example, if I play it with a friend, we're not only trying on the sport and alternate identities (as world-class snowboarders), we're also having fun together—racing past one another on the virtual slopes and doing tricks (and surviving spectacular wipeouts) for one another's benefit. Games are unique among media in allowing us to have this active experience together.

This chapter introduces three building blocks designers use in social digital games to evoke rich emotional responses in players: coordinated action, role-play, and social situations.

Coordinated Action

There is something deeply satisfying and bonding about overcoming a challenging mental and physical situation with someone else, especially if it requires close coordination. If you've ever played team sports, or found yourself in an impromptu collaborative situation (getting a car out of a snowdrift, rescuing someone's wind-scattered papers), then you know these feelings. Social psychologists have demonstrated that giving people opportunities for coordinated action (like asking them to lift and carry boards together) leads to greater feelings of connectedness, mutual liking, and rapport.[7] Games can facilitate this kind of collaboration over an extended period of time, spanning hours, weeks, even years.

The Sony Playstation 3 game *Little Big Planet* showcases the simple pleasures of coordinated action with an elegant set of

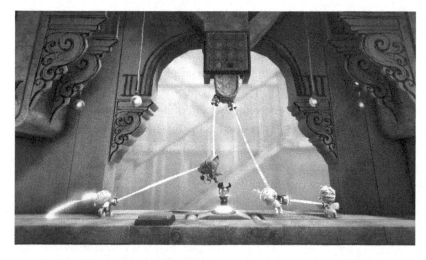

Figure 2.1
Little Big Planet players coordinate avatar actions to solve puzzles.
Source: LittleBigPlanet 2 (MediaMolecule, 2011)

design choices. Launched in 2008, the game was in its third release, in 2014, and still going strong. *Little Big Planet* is a puzzle-platformer, a game genre in which player avatars solve physical puzzles in a two-dimensional world of platforms (see figure 2.1). The avatars can take a simple set of actions—running, jumping, pushing, and pulling—in a world seemingly made of fabric and paper. While the game's look and feel resemble a child's craft project, its sophisticated physics engine makes objects behave more realistically than in other platformer games (e.g., an object sliding down a hill will gain speed until it collides with something or the slope changes).

Players build avatars from a simple base body referred to as "Sackboy," decorating these simple bodies with costuming elements and "stickers" (see figure 2.2). In an unusual twist, *Little*

Figure 2.2
Little Big Planet avatars are built upon a base avatar body known as "Sack-boy." Players have a great deal of latitude in customizing the figure with costuming elements and "stickers."
Source: LittleBigPlanet 2 (MediaMolecule, 2011); image taken from Wikipedia

a

b

Figure 2.3a, b

Happy, very happy, sad, more sad, saddest, and angry expressions for Sackboy, which can be controlled by the player using the D-pad on the game controller.

Source: LittleBigPlanet (MediaMolecule, 2008); image courtesy of H2-Blog

Big Planet lets players puppet the avatar's face and body to convey emotions. Players can adjust the character's happiness, fear, sadness, and anger using the Directional pad (D-pad) on the controller (see figure 2.3a, b; see also a brief online tutorial on puppeteering the avatar).[8] Trigger buttons and tilt controls let players move, gesture, and even slap other players' avatars.

The avatar customization tools and expression controls make these characters feel like handcrafted puppets that the player is both operating and inhabiting in the game world. Unlike the Sims, sack creatures never speak—they express themselves only through their broad body language and facial expressions (not unlike comic silent film actors—see figure 2.4). The game's physics allow for physical antics and complex physical puzzle solving that make the avatars feel expressive and realistic to players despite their simplified bodies.

Little Big Planet encourages social play by design. The game can handle up to four players, either local (i.e., everyone is in the same room, watching the same screen) or online (connected from different locales and screens through the Sony PlayStation network). Some of the puzzles in every level can only be solved through the cooperation of two or more players.

Players solve puzzles physically (and through side conversation if they are in the same room), figuring out whose avatar needs to stand where, or press on what, in order to solve the problem. Players can use the avatars' ready emoting to give one another silent commentary on how things are going, and can physically ham up victory and defeat (figure 2.5).

As one writer describes his play experience:

Helen calls them the "Hurrah!" buttons. L2 + R2 + both analog sticks held upwards. Whenever she wins the most points on a *Little Big Planet* level, she presses these buttons, and her grinning Sackgirl lifts both arms in the air in wordless celebration. My Sackboy, meanwhile, tends to scowl and storm off the side of the screen, fists clenched. Or, after a particularly stressful level, he might pull out a frying pan and hit Helen's Sackgirl over the head. Helen tends to take losing slightly better. She will drag my Sackboy away from the camera, mid-disco dance, in a vain attempt to take the spotlight. Either way, nigh every level ends in a comical scuffle between our characters without a word spoken between us in the real world.[9]

SAFETY LAST

Figure 2.4
Little Big Planet's avatars and game mechanics evoke the classic physical humor and sense of adventure and risk of silent film stars like Harold Lloyd.
Source: Safety Last! (Hal Roach Studios, 1928)

Figure 2.5
Players can make avatars ham it up with facial expressions and broad body language.
Source: Little Big Planet "Sackzilla" trailer, YouTube ("calculatorboyqwe")/ MediaMolecule (2008)

This same writer notes that the controls in *Little Big Planet* allow for rich nonverbal communication between players, immersing them more thoroughly into their characters and the game world: "Instead of Helen telling me to 'go over there,' and pointing at a corner of the television screen, Helen's Sackgirl herself points at a switch within the world and my Sackboy goes there. When he finds the wrong switch, Sackgirl shakes her head angrily and points again. This time my Sackboy gets it right, and Sackgirl grins and gives a thumb up."[10]

The original game shipped with many wildly creative pre-built levels, but the enduring popularity and power of the game derives from the ability to make and share custom levels, including avatar designs. A simple in-game movie showing a player creating a "Sackzilla" and "terrorizing" a city before being defeated by other players[11] shows the range of character styles and emotions that players can put together to create compelling and entertaining scenarios. Anyone can easily download player-created levels and invite others to play. For further customization, *Little Big Planet*, like *The Sims*, offers popular content packs with avatar accessories and costumes ranging from pirates to historical figures to Norse gods.

Little Big Planet's design choices—simple and emotionally puppeteer-able avatars, interesting physics, limited group size, puzzles that require teamwork—create a fun form of coordinated action. These choices also set the emotional tone by delimiting which actions are possible. Simple, comical avatars with controls that make physical antics and comedic interaction easy help lead players into a friendly and silly shared emotional experience as they work together.

Social Avatars and Role-Play

As we saw in chapter 1, avatars enhance emotional experience in solo play. This is even more true in multiplayer situations. When people play together as avatars, the game transforms from a private, personal journey into real social interaction.

Taking on a virtual self in a multiplayer setting brings the gaze and expectations of other players to bear on a player's adopted in-game identity. When I perform another self in the presence of other people, all of us are engaged in actual real-time social interaction taking place through the lens of this playacting. At the same time, we are also immersed in our own role performance viscerally and cognitively. This opens up the possibility for powerful emotional experiences that arise out of a co-performance of roles while engaging in rich, genuine shared experiences. Game designers combine avatars and actions to generate rich possibility spaces for emotionally meaningful social interaction. The game worlds they create may be imaginary, but the social dynamics are not.

In everyday life, human beings inhabit and perform myriad social roles—sister, parent, coworker, student, lover, house guest—as the situation and others around us demand. Sociologist Erving Goffman observed that people enact performances of these roles, presenting the self in a social context toward the outcomes they desire.[12] For example, we may put on a happy face when visiting neighbors, regardless of how we're actually feeling, so as to properly enact the polite visitor. This is not to say that all our social roles are arbitrarily and freely chosen. In fact social roles usually shape and constrain individual behavior, creating a more manageable experience for everyone. The roles we can inhabit in the "real" world are profoundly shaped by many factors, including inborn characteristics, family environment, professional training, and the relationships we have and intend to maintain. Game avatars allow us to peel away some of these layers and adopt alternative identities.[13]

Even in this era of advanced graphics, the most malleable material for digitally crafting identity and social interaction is still text. As we saw in chapter 1, in the case of *Planetfall*'s Floyd, a few well-chosen words can form a rich and eloquent description of an environment or character. If a game world is built to allow for a lot of player customization in avatars, text can make complex identity construction and role-play possible. Text-based

MUDs (Multi-User Dungeons) take advantage of these characteristics of text to provide a rich shared imaginative world for players.

While MUDs have existed since the 1970s, the player base of these games expanded broadly for a time in the early 1990s, as college campuses gave students network access and public awareness of the Internet grew. In a MUD or MOO (Multi-User Dungeons, Object Oriented), players forge their avatars and the virtual environment they inhabit through rich descriptive text. Here, for example, is what you might read as you enter the long-running LambaMOO:

The Coat Closet. The Closet is a dark, cramped space. It appears to be very crowded in here; you keep bumping into what feels like coats, books and other people (apparently sleeping). One useful thing that you've discovered in your bumbling about is a metal doorknob set at waist level into what might be a door. There's a new edition of the newspaper. Type "news" to see it.[14]

By writing verbal descriptions others can view, players can create just about any kind of persona for themselves in these text-based worlds. As one player said in Sherry Turkle's 1995 book:

You can be whoever you want to be. You can completely redefine yourself if you want. You can be the opposite sex. You can be more talkative. You can be less talkative. Whatever. You can just be whoever you want, really, whoever you have the capacity to be. You don't have to worry about the slots other people put you in as much. It's easier to change the way people perceive you, because all they've got is what you show them. They don't look at your body and make assumptions. They don't hear your accent and make assumptions. All they see is your words. And it's always there. Twenty-four hours a day you can walk down to the street corner and there's gonna be a few people there who are interesting to talk to, if you've found the right MUD for you.[15]

Turkle's research showed that people do serious emotional and social work as they play in these environments. One girl who lost part of her leg in a car accident created a character in a MUD who was also missing a leg. She described the character's disability and her prosthesis front and center in the description other players saw upon meeting her.

This meant that everyone who befriended her character in the MUD worked through any issues they might have with her handicap. This included someone that the girl became romantically involved within the MUD. As Turkle puts it:

She and her virtual lover acknowledged the "physical" as well as the emotional aspects of the virtual amputation and prosthesis. They became comfortable with making virtual love, and Ava found a way to love her own virtual body. Ava told the group at the town meeting that this experience enabled her to take a further step toward accepting her real body. "After the accident, I made love in the MUD before I made love again in real life," she said. "I think that the first made the second possible. I began to think of myself as whole again."[16]

While MUDs and MOOs leverage the flexibility of text, more recently designed multiplayer online games take advantage of the power of graphics and physics to frame deeply immersive avatar-based role-play experiences for players. In *City of Heroes*, a massively multiplayer online role-playing game (MMORPG or MMO) that ran from 2004 to 2012, players took on comic-book-style superhero identities. If you ever played superhero as a kid (I personally remember whirling in front of my mirror hoping to transform like my hero, Wonder Woman), you'll understand the appeal of this game.

City of Heroes offered players the chance to create and then inhabit and enact their very own superhero within the game, battling criminals and saving the world alongside other players/superheroes.

The game's designers built a multilayered avatar customization system that made creating a superhero identity a much deeper process than simply choosing a costume. The players' possible choices were closely tied to the core gameplay action, so they could truly *have* superpowers within the gameplay context. *City of Heroes* provided four sets of avatar-creation choices. The first two tied tightly to gameplay features built into the game engine. The second two had no impact on the game's behavior, but plenty of impact on other players' responses.

First, the player chose between five main character archetypes. MMO games typically make players choose a "class" of character to begin with when crafting an avatar (e.g., wizard, healer, warrior, etc., in a fantasy game). These different classes have different sorts of powers in the game world that work well together in group play. In some ways, classes resemble positions on a sports team. In soccer, you have players on offense and defense, subdivided into specialized roles. In MMO games, like soccer, people gravitate toward positions that suit their abilities, style of play, and enthusiasm for certain kinds of tasks in the game. *City of Heroes* players could choose from five main character classes (referred to as archetypes in the game): Blasters (strong fighters), Scrappers (great at close quarters, melee-style combat), and defensive specialist Controllers, Defenders, and Tankers.

After choosing an archetype, the player selected from one of five origin stories: science, mutation, magic, technology, and natural. The origin affected what sorts of enhancements the player could acquire and the types of enemies she was most likely to face. For example, if the player chose the science origin story, her story, though customizable, would follow this general scenario from the game:

You received your powers either through purposeful scientific inquiry or some accident gone awry. You have since learned to harness your new-found abilities, becoming a powerful force in the world. This origin will give you access to Tranq Dart. This item has a very short range and deals minor Lethal and Toxic damage. In addition there is a small chance you can put the target to Sleep with this dart, but they will wake up the next time they are damaged or healed.

A player with the science origin would have access to training, invention, genetic alteration, and experiment enhancements as gameplay progressed.

In contrast, the technology origin overview read as follows:

You derive your powers from technological devices, from suits of high-tech body armor to powerful energy weapons. Few have been able to duplicate the amazing technology that lies behind your gadgets. You need not be a brilliant inventor; you may have acquired these items from another source. This Origin will give you access to Taser Dart. This attack has a very short range and does minor Energy damage. In addition it has a small chance to Hold your opponent for a brief moment.

Enhancements available with this origin choice included training, gadget, invention, and cybernetic.

These overviews show the interweaving of high concept and concrete implications for gameplay. The game designers walked the player through the process of coupling fantasy backstory with pragmatic implications of avatar choices on abilities and likely gameplay outcomes. From here, the player selected one primary power set (such as broadsword, claws, or katana) and one primary power for that set (such as nimble slash or sweeping strike, two possible powers for the dual blade primary power set). These powers were just the start for the player, who could progress through gameplay to acquire more and more strength and ability, as well as enhancements based upon the Origin story that was selected.

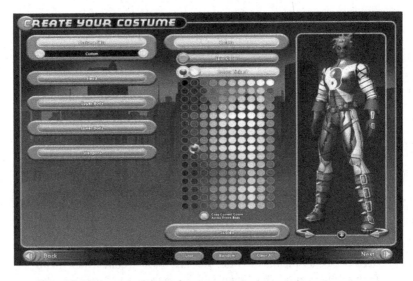

Figure 2.6
Customizing the avatar's costume for *City of Heroes*.
Source: City of Heroes, Venturebeat ("Layton Shumway")/NCSOFT (2010)

After making these gameplay-relevant choices, the player could select from a tremendous range of appearances (see figure 2.6), choosing gender (male, female, or "huge"), height, weight, features, and a detailed variety of costumes. In the last phase of avatar creation, the player registered the avatar, making a final set of choices, including a battle cry and a character description for other players to read.

This deep set of avatar choices gave tremendous latitude to players in crafting their own fantasy figures. As one player puts it, the variety of options and ability to author an origin story "made my CoH characters seem like *my* characters, not some generic gear clotheshorse constructed out of a handful of possible hair and body options."[17] Another notes: "Oh man. The origins you could write in. . . . I ran into random players, and reading their origins, just instantly hit it off, and had great, memorable missions—or even just *conversations*—that I still remember."[18]

When the game was closing down, nostalgic players gathered on forums to share stories about their in-game time. One thread included players' favorite character descriptions.[19] Here are a few examples demonstrating the humor, creativity, and ingenuity players applied in their choices:

• "The Killustrated Man: Who had a lot of tattoos and was good at martial arts."

• "Regina Dentata: The queen of teeth."

• "Organised Mime: He was an evil mime who was super strong and awesome to play."

• "The Hundred Acre Hood: oh bother."

• "Drach Terra: Very colourful demon from a dimension of law and order."

• "Melissa Kane: Formerly a teacher in a school for superpowered children. Now a Revenant out for Revenge."

• "Thunderblitz: Psychotic and Omnicidal Cyborg made from the DNA of a narcissistic supervillain, steampunk technology and powered by an arcane reactor stolen from the Circle of Thorns."

• "That Other Kid: Stuntman who after too many knocks on the head believes that she's actually a super hero. Runs around Paragon City waving a Katana and quoting Quentin Tarantino movies."

• "Swamp Fever: A scientist who merged himself with hallucinogenic swamp plants."

- "I remember in CoV I had a guy in a white suit with White hair and a beard/moustache combo with chicken legs simply called 'The Colonel.'"
- "My first char ever was Miss Information, a villainous secretary out to bring down terrible executives who abused their powers. Then I made Strychnina, and was playing her until GW2 came out. She was a Russian scientist who accidently spliced plant genes into herself and became an angry poisonous woman (no one would love her):)."

Figure 2.7a, b shows some examples of player-created avatars shared on forums about the game. Figure 2.8 shows one of many in-game costume contests the game developers held for players.

In addition to the extensive set of avatar customization choices, the game's developers provided detailed backstory and related tasks and challenges, updating and extending them during the years of the game's run, to activate players and unite them in their adventures in Paragon City. This lore included a rich cast of characters, some inhabited and performed in-game by the company founders. The company even produced special edition comic books released alongside the game. As one player put it: "One of the best things about this game was the lore, how in-depth it was and how different, seemingly disparate storylines ended up linking back together the more you learned about the origin of the NPC heroes and villains."[20]

Players could also author their own missions and story arcs, using the mission architect feature. The game offered multiple ways to have group adventures—players could form leagues and task forces, and also use a sidekick feature in which one player joined with another to play together regardless of their level of mastery in the game. *City of Heroes* also featured cross-server

a

b

Figure 2.7a, b

City of Heroes players were able to create a tremendous range of avatars to support their superhero fantasies.

Source: City of Heroes (Cryptic Studios, 2004); screenshots courtesy of NCSOFT

Figure 2.8
City of Heroes in-game costume contest.
Source: City of Heroes, YouTube ("NCsoft's Official City of Heroes Video Channel")/NCSOFT (2012)

chat, a rarity in MMOs. (This meant that a player logged into the game could chat with any other player logged into the game, even if their play was taking place on a different server.)

The combination of all these features contributed to players' emotional and social engagement—deep avatar customizability linked integrally to gameplay and framed with a rich and evolving backstory, and a variety of ways to play together and stay connected. The designers of *City of Heroes* made the most of the MMO format and its capabilities, to provide players with an engaging shared superhero experience. Players remarked on how well the game delivered on the superhero premise: "That was what I really loved about CoH. They made the powers really feel unique and tried their best to give you the real, full benefits of them and make you feel like a super hero." "One of the best memories was running this mission with an impromptu super group, all exchanging stories of how we got our costumes while beating up thugs in a junkyard. Whoever said that writing your own character's backstory for others to read was the best was right. So much fun."[21]

City of Heroes brought the superhero myth to gamers in a dynamic way interwoven with their social lives both in and out of game. One player remarked: "City of Heroes was how I met my best friend. We met talking about it at lunch in jr. high." Ironically, another remarked: "When I first heard about this game my friends and I wanted to play it so bad we ran around the school yard pretending to be superheroes."[22] As with many MMOs, devoted players logged many hours of their time in the game, playing for years, sometimes with the same people. At the shutting down of the game's servers in 2012, one player dove in for a last round and posted:

Well. That's it. City of Heroes is done as of about five minutes ago. I was there for the end, and I'm glad. It's like visiting a relative on their deathbed; I really, really, didn't want to, but I'm already glad I did. A friend I'd made in the game and played with seven years ago—seven years ago—was on with her original character. We chatted and traded Facebook info. I used to help her with her math homework. Turns out she's married now, to a dude she met in the game. She doesn't MMO much anymore, but at least now we can keep in touch. I was there on the first day and the last. It feels right, I guess, as right as anything can.[23]

Social Situations

When creating multiplayer games, designers act as social engineers—using game elements to create social situations that are interesting and compelling, scenarios where players have fun *together*. Psychologists, most notably Walter Mischel, have long pointed out the powerful influence of social situations on the way individual personalities show themselves.[24] Game designers set up situations aimed at bringing certain kinds of actions and impulses to the fore, thus creating the emotional and social responses that they would like people to experience together. Some game designers take an active ethical stance toward cultivating certain kinds of social situations and desired outcomes for players that reflect their values.[25]

For example, Anna Antropy's *Keep Me Occupied* (figures 2.9a, b and 2.10), created for the 2012 Occupy Oakland movement, was carefully crafted to reflect and enhance movement participants' aim of building upon one another's efforts toward the common good.

Antropy explained in a post that she designed *Keep Me Occupied* as an arcade-style cabinet game intended to go in an abandoned building that the movement planned to occupy; the cabinet had wheels and would travel around Oakland when not in the building. She wanted a game where every player would contribute to the collective success of the group. She describes her idea as follows:

The two players are working together to get as high as they can in sixty seconds. when the sixty seconds are up, each player leaves her avatar behind to stand on the last switch she touched, holding it open for everyone who plays the game afterward. (every player gets a different color so she can recognize her avatar later.) as more and more gates are permanently opened, it's easier for players to get farther in the sixty second time limit. what was important to me was that even less-skilled players could contribute—they might only make it as far as an early set of switches, but because more successful players hadn't occupied those switches yet, these players could hold them down and save all future players the time they would have otherwise spent on them. i also liked players having the choice of making voluntary sacrifices to help future players, so i included shortcuts that allowed players to bypass big portions of the game, but required a player to opt out of advancing upwards in favor of occupying the switch.[26]

a

b

Figure 2.9a, b
Players of *Keep Me Occupied* (a game built and deployed during the Occupy Oakland movement in 2012).
Source: Shaun Roberts (www.shaunroberts.net) (2012)

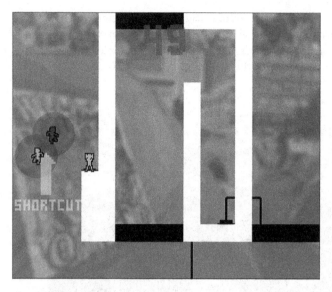

Figure 2.10
Each player is assigned a unique avatar color in the game, so that they can find themselves in the game state later. Players work together to open gates, and past players' avatars are left behind holding open gates for others so they can build upon the work of those who went before them.
Source: Keep Me Occupied (freeware, 2012); image courtesy of Anna Anthropy

About forty people were able to play the game before a very violent police crackdown on the marchers that made the international news. They never made it into the buildings they intended to occupy. The protestors pushed the heavy arcade cabinet along with them and, when the march regrouped, put it away in the sound truck for another day.

Keep Me Occupied is easy to play, and the cumulative and collective nature of the experience is unique. The simple avatars encourage ready and universal identification, and yet the individual coloring allows players to go back and see their contribution to the whole. The task is easy to grasp, the controls familiar, and the feel of the game is (literally) uplifting (the characters soar ever higher in the level as they open gates). Play cycles are very short—sixty seconds—and the arcade cabinet provides a familiar play context visible from afar, encouraging spectators and turn-taking. *Keep Me Occupied* shows how minimal design and a clear emotional goal can create a desired end experience for players. Antropy made a series of savvy design decisions to craft a social situation for players that mirrored their hopes and aspirations for their social movement work.

City of Heroes also offers a designed social situation. Players craft superhero personas and play out their superpower fantasies within the parameters provided. The missions, the lore, and the progression of powers all help guide their performance—to keep it in "bounds." Along the way they get to know other players, and form affections for, and connections to, them based on shared in-game activities. The designed social situation is heroic and epic, in the tradition of the comic book fantasies upon which the game is based.

But designer intentions and programmed boundaries can be warped and even actively transgressed. Players have always enjoyed exploring these limits. Indeed, this can be an integral part of the joy of play.[27] Designers of MMOs stress the importance of working with players as they explore and renegotiate what is possible and desirable in play.[28] Sometimes players ferret out an imbalance in the inherent powers of the avatars, and vote with their feet, or exploit certain reward systems in ways that may force the game to change.

Such changes can sometimes lead to serious conflicts within a game community. New Orleans researcher David Myers[29] had been playing *City of Heroes* for quite some time, and had an advanced character named Twixt who was reasonably well known and respected. The developers of the game introduced a new PvP (player versus player) scenario available only to advanced players. As Myers puts it: "It became increasingly evident that these newly competitive play elements opposed and, in the opposition, revealed the game's cooperative play norms. In a sense, by introducing PvP competition, the designers of *CoH/V* had Garfinkeled their game. I further explored this with Twixt."

What Myers means here by "Garfinkeling" is a technique originated by sociologist Harold Garfinkel. Garfinkel and his students studied the creation and preservation of social order. They conducted "breaching experiments," where they would violate social norms—by, perhaps, standing very close to a conversation partner, or bargaining in a department store—and observe how people tried to repair or restore order.

To Garfinkel *City of Heroes*, Myers violated the game's well-established norms of cooperation and collaboration by following the exact letter of the new PvP mode without acknowledging or deferring to the social rules that had emerged in the larger game community. For instance, rather than giving opponents a sporting chance, he might use his powers to transport opponents to a robot firing line where they had no chance of fighting back or surviving. As he explained, "At first, my interest was solely in adapting and perfecting Twixt's play to accomplish the PvP game goals. I did not expect anything like the severity—or the ferocity—of what occurred as a result."[30]

Twixt's opponents took enormous offense at what was perceived as his antisocial behavior. In addition to denigrating Twixt as a coward on chat servers, they repeatedly appealed to game moderators to kick Twixt off the game. They derided him as a low-skilled player, despite his high ranks and stats: in fact, players persisted in denying Twixt's skill even when confronted with logs from the game. Twixt's own in-game group expelled him for his behavior, despite their long-standing play relationship. He even received a sort of death threat: "10-09-2006 [*Broadcast*] i swear if i ever meet you i will physically kill you for real."

Myers found this violent and sustained social reaction to his in-game behavior fascinating, as it revealed a strong player culture of cooperative play even when faced with new rules, competitive elements, and rewards structures. Although a more competitive, individual-focused play atmosphere had proven appealing in many other MMOs, in this case, players rose up to protect the communal feel of the gameplay that had emerged among them over time. One might say that the initial social situation of *City of Heroes*—communal, heroic behavior—took on a sustained life of its own in players' behavior and expectations, one that overrode the designers' subsequent attempts to tune or tweak the game's social experience. Players had developed personas and shared memories of role-playing under certain rules, official or otherwise, and did not want to upend this shared history in the more advanced, more competitive levels of play.

Wrapping Up

In multiplayer gaming, the meaningful actions that make up each individual's gameplay experience combine to create real social experiences between players, despite the "virtual" nature of the world they find themselves in. Designers leverage the emotional heft of coordinated action and expression in games like *Little Big Planet*. They provide rich tools for engaging in social role-play using avatars, as we saw in *City of Heroes*. And they craft social situations to cultivate certain kinds of social and emotional experiences for players, as in *Keep Me Occupied*.

Avatars in multiplayer contexts allow people to explore fantasy identities and powers, and to enact them with one another over time, sharing what are in fact "real" experiences. The hybrid nature of these experiences, which are both virtual and real, brings a social charm of its own. Consider, for example, the slapstick nonverbal interactions between Helen and Brendon (described above) in *Little Big Planet*.[31] Or the delight in peeking at another player's backstory in *City of Heroes* and striking up a conversation that leads to a lasting friendship.

These examples and others in this chapter (from trying on life with a missing limb to vehemently protecting a valued game culture) clearly demonstrate how players can become highly engaged, even transformed, when they inhabit avatars and interact in social gameplay, however artificial and fantastic their digital "virtual" surroundings may be. Game designers are, in effect, molding our social milieu and the way we build ties with one another, as well as shaping how we see ourselves.

They are also providing us with contexts for forming real and meaningful relationships through role-play that can somehow become part of a person's lasting identity. As game researcher and designer Celia Pearce describes her relationship with an avatar she named Artemisia:

When I log off of these worlds—when I untransform, or retransform, from Artemisia to Celia—Artemesia pops off the screen. The screen image of the various "mes" dissolves like a bubble, but Artemesia still exists inside Celia: she is still part of the complex of mes that is both Celia and Artemesia. . . .

. . . I, as Artemesia, am also present to others when I am not in-world. I am in their memories, remembered, referred to, imagined; thus, in some sense, I remain "real," even when I am not present, for those who have seen and played with me online. . . . We who inhabit avatars all know each other in this way. We can hold multiple identities both within ourselves and in our conceptions of each other.[32]

I would argue that no other medium offers this kind of transformative power at the individual and social levels. And game designers continue to push the boundaries of their medium to artfully frame players' explorations of their interconnected identities, as we'll see in the next two chapters.

3 Bodies at Play: Using Movement Design to Create Emotion and Connection

Remember the lone gamer stereotype from chapter 2? The player you envisioned probably sat hunched over a keyboard or a game controller, focused intently on a screen, the only signs of life his frantically twitching fingers, and his rare outbursts of joy or frustration (figure 3.1a, b).

Though it's true that most people still play games "the old-fashioned way," sitting in front of screens with handheld controllers, game designers have been shaking things up—literally. In the last few years, both independent and mainstream commercial games have started incorporating the vigorous, coordinated movement of bodies as a key element of gameplay.

There's nothing necessarily wrong with sitting down, focusing hard, and using one's hands. In fact, modern schooling and office work depends on just that, as does much problem solving and many creative pursuits (puzzles, fixing things, needlework, writing). Rather, it's a matter of degree. Health researchers warn that we need to move more in daily life,[1] a mandate game designers have taken seriously, despite (or perhaps because?) of the blame they've taken for an epidemic of sedentary youth. In fact, game designers and developers are at the vanguard of innovating new styles of bodily engagement,[2] and they're exploring

Figure 3.1a, b

Robbie Cooper captures the faraway stares of kids focusing on gameplay. *Source:* Robbie Cooper, *Immersion*, New York Times Magazine video, 3:47, November 21, 2008, http://www.nytimes.com/video/magazine/1194833565213/immersion.html

new emotional terrain in the process. In this chapter, we'll look at the striking impact that movements of the body can have on players' emotional and social experience. I've focused much of my own research in the last few years on understanding how movement impacts players,[3] so in this chapter, you'll see many examples from the work we do in my lab.

I'll start with an overview of how and why movement directly impacts emotion, then show three ways game designers use movement to shape emotion and social connection—setting up physical challenges that provoke emotional responses, using movement to catalyze interesting social dynamics, and using the body as a vehicle for bringing players' fantasy identities to life.

Motion and Emotion

Researchers have designed some clever strategies for figuring out how our body affects our emotions. In one study, for instance, researchers had subjects hold a pencil between their teeth in one of two ways while completing various tasks: either with their lips pursed around the pencil (activating frown muscles in the face), or with their teeth clenched around it (activating smile muscles in the face). Subjects with the pencil in the teeth clenched/smile position said they liked the task more than the group with the pursed lips/frown position.[4] A person's body posture can also affect his or her feelings. As social psychologist Amy Cuddy of Harvard explains in one of the most downloaded TED talks (24 million views), if I strike a "high-power" pose for a couple of minutes versus a "low-power pose" (see figure 3.2), then not only will I report feeling more powerful, but my body chemistry will also shift, producing more testosterone and less cortisol—a sign of lowered stress level.[5]

High-power poses   Low-power poses

Figure 3.2
High-power and low-power poses affect a person's self-reported attitude, as well as body chemistry and risk-taking behavior.
Source: Illustration courtesy of Jason Lee (originally appeared in J. Cloud, "Strike a Pose," *Time*, November 10, 2010, http://content.time.com/time/magazine/article/0,9171,2032113,00.html)

Body-based emotional effects give game designers additional options for affecting players' emotions. Kids use these effects intuitively on the playground. A pretend swordfight feels much more intense if you act it out with fake swords than if you sit on the floor with your friends knocking Playmobil knights together. When you swing and parry and duck and cover for real, you feel it more both in your body and your mind. You're using your body to amp up the play experience.

Over the past ten years, every major gaming console device began offering movement-tracking hardware add-ons. Nintendo started the trend in 2006 with the Wiimote—a handheld controller that tracked motion using embedded sensors. In 2010, Sony introduced the Move, and Microsoft, the Kinect. These widely available devices make it possible for game designers to spark feelings in players by getting them to perform certain movements as a part of gameplay. If the game requires that I move around frantically, my brain will pick up my body's physical

Figure 3.3
Wii Sports boxing encourages frantic movement from players, which creates a high-energy experience for them emotionally, in part as a result of their own movement.
Source: Photo courtesy of Lindsay Fincher (2008)

signals and I will actually start to feel somewhat frantic. For example, *Wii Sports* boxing (see figure 3.3) encourages frenetic movement, which in turn creates a feeling of excitement and high energy in players.[6] Likewise, *Star Wars: The Force Unleashed,* lets players use physical motions to hurl on-screen enemies into the air and across the room with a simple and elegant flick of the Wii remote (figure 3.4a, b). After studying games like this, researchers have found that player emotions are in fact different

Figure 3.4a, b

Star Wars: The Force Unleashed used the Wiimote and Nunchuk movement controllers to allow players to "use the force" like Jedi knights. Here, the player raises several enemies with a gesture (https://www.youtube.com/watch?v=VuzFzs0hPKc).

Source: Star Wars: The Force Unleashed fan trailer, YouTube ("TNTv")/LucasArts (2007)

during movement-based play than during controller-based play,[7] and have begun to explore more systematically what sorts of movement styles lead to what sorts of feelings.[8]

Not only do our movements shape our own emotions, but they also affect anyone who's watching us—emotions are, in a sense, "contagious."[9] Our brains are predisposed to pick up and join in the emotions of other people. Neuroscientists have observed that certain neurons in our brains fire when we simply *watch* movement others make; these same neurons in our own brains fire when we make similar movements ourselves.[10] In other words, our brains seem to simulate what the other person is doing *and* feeling, running their actions and reactions through our mind, in the same way that we rehearse or perform our own actions. Conversely, other research looks at what happens when a person *can't* physically imitate someone else's movements, however subtly. One study found that people injected with Botox were not as sensitive to facial expression of emotion as people who had not been injected,[11] presumably because they could not move their own faces in sympathy with the faces of others they were trying to "read."

Emotional contagion based on body movements offers two advantages to game designers looking to shape how players feel. First, anybody watching someone play will pick up on and (to some extent) share the emotions that the player acts out physically. This can cause an emotional snowball effect in a room where body-based social gameplay is happening. You can see this reflected in the faces of the spectators in figure 3.3. Second, avatars and NPCs can be leveraged to create feelings in players. If an on-screen character physically demonstrates signs of emotions, the designer can assume the player will pick those up and feel them to some extent as well.

Figure 3.5
Player avatars from *Dance Central 2*.
Source: Dance Central 2 (Microsoft Studios, 2011); screenshot courtesy of Shacknews

For example, at the 2011 Game Developers Conference,[12] designers Dean Tate and Matt Boch described the many prototypes the team tested before coming up with the final version of their hit game, *Dance Central*. One version used the camera on the Kinect device to capture video of players dancing, and put that video on the screen so it looked as if players were really dancing in the game. It quickly became evident, however, that people didn't like seeing themselves on-screen. They grew self-conscious and fixated on the awkward moves they made while learning new steps.

The designers realized it was better to eliminate the video and instead show a confident, smooth avatar representing the player on-screen (see figure 3.5). Essentially, the dancing avatar projected poise and confidence, and these "contagious" states "infected" players and boosted their own confidence.

In this and other examples we'll see, designers intuitively draw on what is known about emotions, the body, the brain, and social situations in order to deploy tools and strategies to shape player emotion. These strategies range from presenting satisfying levels of physical challenge, to evoking a bond between people through creating shared physical tasks, to the use of role-playing to generate new emotions and let players try on alternate identities. Body-based design broadens the emotional possibility space of games.

Physical Challenges: Mastering the Body

As we covered in chapter 1, great games keep players just at the edge of their skill level in an optimal, "flow" state. This doesn't happen by accident: designers artfully prepare and precisely dispense challenges to create an engaging experience. The ability to use the entire body for gameplay lets designers harness additional emotional power not possible in sedentary, hand-controlled games. It also adds another level of pleasure for players, by adding more complex and difficult challenges and rewards. Learning to master complex movements engaging the whole body brings a physical and mental pleasure that athletes and dancers know well. Intense physical activity itself can release chemicals in the body that produce a "high."[13]

Increasingly, movement game designers are taking these effects into account to design compelling and sometimes surprising experiences for players.[14] For instance, when *Dance Dance Revolution* (*DDR*) swept college campuses a decade ago, it ended up delivering more than just a quirky and compelling game experience: it actually reshaped bodies. Many students reported weight loss after joining campus clubs or playing a lot in arcades and at home.[15] Studies reported that sedentary teenagers who played *DDR* for a while changed their attitudes about exercise and fitness.[16]

The impact of games on the body can extend to a wider range of experiences than amped up excitement and intensity. Relaxation and calmness are as deeply intertwined with the mind and body as agitation and excitement: calming the breath can tame one's emotional landscape as well. In the Kinect-based game *Leela*, for example, the "Stillness Meditation" module uses the Kinect's camera and depth sensors to give players visual feedback on their breathing, nudging them toward fuller and more relaxed breath cycles (see figure 3.6).

Many other games have also used bodily motion and breathing to drive a calming and meditative play experience, from Char Davies's *Osmose* (1995)[17] to the more recent game *Deep* (2015). *Deep* combines the use of the Occulus Rift virtual reality headset with a custom controller that measures how much the diaphragm expands and contracts. The designer intended the game to quell anxiety in players, having built it as a response to his own struggles with anxiety.

Players seem to find it a powerful and useful tool. Christos Reid, a therapist who tried it at a conference, said:

It was weird—I was trying to watch the game, but I had tears at the bottom of the Oculus headset because it calmed me down more than anything ever has in my entire life. I took it off after five minutes or so and [the designer]'s looking at me —he'd been at the mental health talk and he knew my input was valuable—and asked, 'What do you think?' It was really intense—I just started crying. I was just trying to get the words out because I was so emotional because I had never had such an effective anxiety treatment before. Nothing has ever helped me the way *Deep* did.[18]

Figure 3.6
Visual feedback on breathing during *Leela*'s Stillness Meditation module.
Source: Deepak Chopra, *Leela* (THQ/Curious Pictures, 2011); screenshot courtesy of *Business Insider*

Physical challenges from games don't always require special hardware. In the cult game *Desert Bus*, created by magicians Penn and Teller during the CD-ROM boom and never officially released,[19] players use keyboard controls to simulate driving a bus through a desert for hours on end, which turns out to be physically and mentally grueling (see figure 3.7).

As *New Yorker* reviewer Simon Parkin puts it:

Finishing a single leg of the trip requires considerable stamina and concentration in the face of arch boredom: the vehicle constantly lists to the right, so players cannot take their hands off the virtual wheel; swerving from the road will cause the bus's engine to stall, forcing the player to be towed back to the beginning. The game cannot be paused. The bus carries no virtual passengers to add human interest, and there is no traffic to negotiate. The only scenery is the odd sand-pocked rock or road sign. Players earn a single point for each eight-hour trip completed between the two cities, making a Desert Bus high score perhaps the most costly in gaming.[20]

The game was resurrected in 2006 and taken up by a group who decided to raise money by going on marathon "journeys" with it, creating a charity they called Desert Bus for Hope. So far they have raised over a million dollars by holding annual bus driving marathons.[21] Contributors clearly believe that the effort

Figure 3.7
Desert Bus tests players' stamina by requiring them to drive a difficult-to-steer bus through a virtual desert for hours and hours of real-time play.
Source: Desert Bus (Electronic Arts/Absolute Entertainment, 1995); screen-shot courtesy of YouTube ("Phrasz013")

involved in "driving" the bus for hours is as worthy of support as a more obviously physical stamina-based challenge such as a walk-a-thon.

In another keyboard-based experience that makes players acutely aware of physical presence and effort, game designer Pippin Barr collaborated with performance artist Marina Abramović to adapt and extend some of the experiences Abramović offers to those who visit her institute in Hudson, New York. These exercises aim to enhance "your connection with yourself and with the present moment" (verbatim from the game instructions), and the emotional tenor of what unfolds depends upon each player's attitude and approach. As in *Desert Bus*, the activities are deceptively simple and draw attention to small details of one's physical actions. For example, one game requires players to walk their avatars up a ramp using the arrow keys, as slowly as possible (similar to walking meditation). Meanwhile, the player must keep the Shift key pressed down continuously to indicate presence and attention. Curious readers can try these games online.[22] But be ready to devote some time and focus—the site requests players to sign a certificate saying they will commit one hour to the experience, and exercises will time out for an hour if you let go of the Shift key once you begin.

Game artists have also explored a darker facet of physical experience—playing through physical pain and injury. In 2001, artists Eddo Stern and Mark Allen hosted a game tournament they called *Tekken Torture Tournament*. At the time, *Tekken* was the most popular fighting game for the Sony PlayStation. For this tournament, players wore devices that administered electric shocks to their arms (see figure 3.8a, b) when their on-screen avatars took blows. The shocks did not cause permanent damage, but they hurt; they also caused temporary movement

a

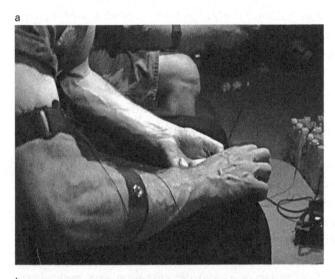

b

Figure 3.8a, b

During the *Tekken Torture Tournament*, electric shocks were administered to player's arms when their on-screen avatars suffered damage.

Source: Tekken Torture Tournament, Eddo Stern (2001)

difficulty that mimicked the delays avatars experience in-game after being dealt a heavy blow. Players had to sign an intimidating release form,[23] but nonetheless enthusiastically participated in the tournament as it toured art venues in the United States, Israel, Australia, and the Netherlands.

German artists Volker Morawe and Tilman Reiff took the exploration of pain and play a step further, creating a game machine that could, in fact, inflict physical harm. Their piece, originally titled *PainStation* but later renamed due to copyright issues with Sony, is a custom-built console (see figure 3.9) where

Figure 3.9
PainStation console, originally built in 2001, with the capacity to inflict wounds upon players.
Source: PainStation, Volker Morawe and Tilman Reiff (2006)

two players compete in a *Pong*-like game.[24] Each player controls his paddle with the right hand, while the left rests on a part of the console the artists deemed the "Pain Execution Unit" (PEU). The PEU could heat up and administer electric shocks. It also contained a small wire whip that would pop out and strike the player's hand, inflicting real physical wounds.

I'll never forget the first time I saw *PainStation* in action. The game was part of an exhibition at a museum in San Francisco, where I was installing an art project I'd collaborated on (SimGallery).[25] During setup, artists and curators were trying out one another's games before the show went live. I watched a round of *PainStation* between the exhibition curator and his assistant curator. It became clear to me that the assistant curator was subtly trying to lose the round, in order to avoid inflicting pain on her manager. The rest of us were watching intently, but also trying not to look too interested in what the outcome would be. We all wanted to maintain our own good relationships with the curation staff, and it was unclear how to spectate tactfully and appropriately. The possibility of physical harm completely altered the human dynamics surrounding the gameplay. It was a mesmerizing and horrifying demonstration of how physical stakes can radically shift the emotional and social tenor of the play experience.

Moving Together: Designing Social Dynamics and Feelings

In chapter 2, I introduced research on the positive emotional effects of coordinated action.[26] Adding physical movement to the designer's palette heightens the impact of player coordination, by layering in emotions that arise through physical feedback and emotional contagion, and also by orchestrating interpersonal distance and interactions between bodies. Researchers can tell a lot about relationships by looking at how closely people stand together, how they arrange themselves, and when and how they touch one another.[27] When designers use movement as a game mechanic, they can reengineer the normal ebb and flow of physical contact, the space between bodies, and the joint coordination of movement for dramatic effect. Movement that puts players' bodies into new or unexpected physical configurations can trigger strong social and emotional experiences. Let's look at ways designers have leveraged these factors in social gameplay situations ranging from pure competition, to blended "coopetition," to pure cooperation.

Pure Competition

In everyday adult life, we learn to keep a polite distance from one another and avoid aggressive contact. Competitive physical games in the digital space can flout these norms to great social and emotional effect. Independent developers have led the way in creating such games, perhaps because commercial developers perceive such social violation as too risky.

The canonical example of a movement game that encourages physical boundary breaking and frantic competition is *J. S. Joust*, created by Douglas Wilson and the Copenhagen Game Collective (see figure 3.10a, b, c). Winner of the Independent Game Festival's Nuovo and Grand Prize awards in 2012, and many other awards, *Joust* uses the Move controller designed for the Sony PlayStation, but players look at each other, not at a screen. In this multiplayer game, two to seven people hold controllers and move about freely to music (Bach's Brandenburg Concertos, which give the game its name), trying not to jar their controllers in the process. Tipping or jostling the controllers triggers a light

Figure 3.10a, b, c
J. S. Joust uses handheld movement controllers without a screen and encourages physical contact and frantic chases. For a look at *J. S. Joust* in action, see Johan Bichel Lindegaard, *Johann Sebastian Joust! at Amager Strandpark*, Vimeo video, 1:09, June 4, 2011, https://vimeo.com/24662278.
Source: Johann Sebastian Joust, Brent Knepper/Sara Bobo/Die Gute Fabrik (2014)

and a loud sound, and the player has to leave the round. The controllers are a little more forgiving when the music is fast, which gives players a brief window to dash at one another. Gameplay can be quite genteel or very rough, depending upon what players are willing to do. Players can gang up on a single player, but in the end, only one player wins. Thus competition can be fierce. Wilson took his inspiration from folk games like egg-and-spoon races,[28] which offer a chance for friends and neighbors to challenge one another and work off energy and tensions in a playful way. And indeed, playing this game feels like an exhilarating and often hilarious combination of tag and an egg-and-spoon race.

Another game using physicality to heighten competition is the 2012 Indiecade finalist *Hit Me!*, by artist and game designer Kaho Abe (see figure 3.11a, b). Players wear helmets equipped with cameras, each with a button on top. Players try to push the button on top of each other's helmets. If they succeed, the camera snaps a picture. A player gets extra points for appearing in the snapshot he or she triggers.

Spectators enjoy this strange and comical form of aggression almost as much as players: after all, in everyday life, we rarely see people trying to bop each other on the head. The designer, Abe, was the resident artist in my lab, and I had graduate students in one of my seminars play the game, which revealed

a

b

Figure 3.11a, b

Hit Me! requires players to press a button on top of one another's heads to gain points. The game brings players into a combative stance they might normally never take toward another person in everyday life. To watch *Hit Me!* in action, see https://vimeo.com/29638917

Source: Hit Me! (Kaho Abe, 2011)

rich and fascinating interpersonal dynamics. As it turned out, a
student's everyday demeanor did not reliably predict their reaction to being asked to (gently) whack another student on the
head against their will. Nor did it predict how students would
go about the task. One very polite student turned out to be a
vigorous and feisty opponent, fearless in her leaping attempts
to press other students' buttons, and extremely comical in her
body language. The funniest matchup was between this student
and a male student who was trained in martial arts. He consistently defeated other men, but, when playing this particular
student, found himself unable to be as hard-driving. All the
matches produced fascinating social negotiations of space and
contact. With its ridiculous helmets and awkward, silly motions
encouraged by the rules, *Hit Me!* comes off as very comical, more
Three Stooges than barroom brawl. Nevertheless, the game feels
like a high-stakes endeavor. In trying to press your opponent's
button, you have to move deeply into their space and leap up
in an odd, exposed sort of way. It feels wacky, awkward, and
socially inappropriate. Abe has adeptly choreographed physical
game mechanics to create this unique mix of feelings in players
and spectators.

"Coopetition"

Mixing competition with collaboration in a single game allows
players to share positive emotion with their own team, and
also enjoy the powerful buzz of group competition. This brand
of social physical play will feel familiar to anyone who's ever
played a sport. Not surprisingly, in fact, movement game designers sometimes mimic sports themselves as they attempt to
evoke the emotional and social work that sports accomplish for
us. Senior Wii bowling leagues are a good example. *Wii Sports*

bowling, distributed with the original Nintendo Wii platform, mimics most of the structure of "real" bowling, including the scoring system. Instead of rolling a real ball down an alley, players use the Wiimote to simulate this action. The game works well for seniors who can't go out and bowl anymore for various reasons. Many players bowled in the past, so they're comfortable with the game's action, controls, and framework; senior Wii bowlers sometimes even extend bowling's traditional social rituals, like team shirts and friendly trash-talking, to the virtual game. Senior Wii bowling leagues (such as the National Senior League[29]) use the Internet to allow teams to compete from a wide geographic area, without ever leaving their centers, which may be impractical or impossible for many of the players. The movement-based play enhances the pleasure and group feeling of the experience for the team members as they rack up scores to send off, and it also increases the excitement for local center spectators cheering them on.

The dance game *Yamove!* also draws on a real-world team-based physical activity, in this case, b-boy/b-girl-style dance battles. Dance battles originated in the 1970s along with rapping and scratching/mixing records, and still thrives today as a competitive form across the world.[30] Crews of dancers compete with each other, with individuals facing off in front of judges. *Yamove!* adapted and modified this format into a dance battle that takes place between *pairs* of players (see figure 3.12a, b). Inspired by the research linking physical coordination with emotional bonding and trust building,[31] the game requires players to improvise moves that showcase both partners' dance skills: the goal is to move well *together*. Pairs, not individuals, receive scores, which reinforces the benefits of collaboration, while teams also experience the excitement of team competition in

Figure 3.12a, b

Yamove, a dance-battle game that challenges pairs to move in synchrony. To see players in action, see https://www.youtube.com/watch?v=N5igt1lX6Bg.

Source: NYU Game Innovation Lab, *Yamove!* (2012)

front of an audience. Each player wears a mobile device (phone or iPod) strapped to his or her forearm, and teams compete in three rounds. Dance pairs aim for high-intensity, in-sync, and diverse dance routines; the devices track movement data and assign scores. Adding to the excitement, a live MC (master of ceremonies, a term for the disc jockey who chooses, blends, and comments on music as he or she plays it) calls out feedback to the players so they know how they're doing. Even though results also appear on a big screen, this is more for spectators than for players. Players are too busy keeping their eyes on each other to coordinate moves and stay in sync. *Yamove!* was a finalist at Indiecade 2012 and was also showcased at the 2012 World Science Festival.[32]

Games like *Yamove!*, *Hit Me!*, and *JS Joust* all have something interesting in common—they avoid using a big screen to provide continuous and extensive feedback to players. Researchers have found that enhanced bonding and mutual good feeling more reliably arises from coordinated physical activity involving mutual gaze.[33] The more players look at each other, the better results they achieve in coordination and the stronger the lingering positive social effects. Thus the more attention players can put on each other's movements, the more effectively the designer can use movement to evoke emotion and drive interesting social configurations and experiences. Indie games like the ones in this chapter use sound, tactile feedback, and human support, in roles such as the MC host, to break away from a reliance on a tight visual coupling of the player with the screen. I believe these kinds of tactics will become more common as our world grows increasingly saturated with sensors and alternate feedback systems beyond big screens.

Pure Cooperation

Purely cooperative physical games ask players to meld their actions and intentions to achieve a common goal. Often these games reconfigure the arrangements of players' bodies, dissolving the traditional spatial bubbles between people and among groups, provoking new emotions and connections.

Bounden (2014), for example, forces reconfiguration of the space between people. The game requires two players, but only one mobile device. Each placing a thumb on the screen, the players must move together to keep a virtual sphere visible and move it through a path of rings by tilting and rotating the device together. The result is (relatively) graceful synchronized movement that was in fact choreographed by the Dutch National Ballet (see figure 3.13). Using this very simple game task, *Bounden's* designers lead players to move together, feel graceful together, and come closer together physically than they otherwise might, thereby evoking increased intimacy and trust.

Ninja Shadow Warrior also leverages physical closeness, encouraging as many people as possible to squeeze together. In this game, housed in a handcrafted arcade cabinet, players under attack in a virtual palace must hide using their "ninja powers" to transform into a vase, a tree, or some other ordinary object. They do so by shaping their bodies to fit a simple silhouetted shape (see figure 3.14a, b, c), displayed on the screen. Because several people can fill out a silhouette better than someone playing solo, the best scores come from group coordination. In this way, the game rewards close physical coordination simply by making it the most successful strategy. The game plays a little like the 1960s parlor game *Twister*, where players contort themselves in close contact with one another. *Ninja Shadow Warrior* pushes a

Figure 3.13
Bounden is a two-player mobile-based game.
Source: Bounden (Game Oven, 2014)

Figure 3.14a, b, c
Ninja Shadow Warrior has players try to form a shape's silhouette without getting any body parts out of bounds.
Source: Ninja Shadow Warrior (Kaho Abe, 2011)

playful form of physical intimacy upon players for a brief game cycle and posts it online in a photo stream. Not surprisingly, you see a lot of engaged and sometimes sheepish smiles on the Ninja Shadow Warrior Tumblr.[34]

This sort of "the more the merrier" cooperative play design (figure 3.15a, b) also drives *Pixel Motion*, a game my lab created as part of a research project that looked at future uses of surveillance cameras. We wanted to explore the notion of surveillance cameras as a public utility: What if everyone had access

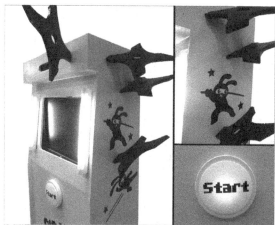

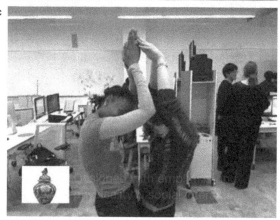

a

b

Figure 3.15a, b
Pixel Motion uses surveillance cameras and motion sensing to create physical collaboration among strangers.
Source: NYU Game Innovation Lab, *Pixel Motion* (2013)

to these cameras that surround us? What might we all do with that power? We worked on this project with researchers from Bell Labs who had developed motion flow software that identified overall movement patterns in video streams. The game was designed for a public museum space, at the Liberty Science Center in Jersey City, New Jersey. We wanted to create an experience that would actually mix strangers together in a common activity, to encourage them to forge connections and have more of a sense of community (most games and interactive experiences in museums have sensors that track only a handful of participants, so typically, one small group after another tries the activity, without much mingling among groups).

In *Pixel Motion*, anyone in the camera's field of view can join in "wiping" pixels off the video feed by moving around within the play space. Players have thirty seconds to wipe off enough pixels to win the round. A win means everyone gets to pose in a photo with on-screen props and share the resulting "postcard" via email or Twitter, creating a lasting memory of the game. The game's leader board features postcard photos from high-scoring games.

The project team studied video and photo streams from the exhibit to understand the flow of groups as they engaged the game. We found that the design of *Pixel Motion* encouraged intergroup collaboration and blurred boundaries between clusters of museumgoers who normally wouldn't mix much.[35] You can see this in the win-screen souvenir photos of victorious players, who tend not to recluster themselves into their own social groups (e.g., figure 3.15b, a souvenir snapshot of players from several visitor groups posing after a win). The game reconfigured the physical space within and around groups of people, mingling them together spatially and thus potentially breaking down social barriers between them as well.

Body and Fantasy Identity

We've seen the emotional power that comes from mastery of a new physical skill, and the social and emotional power that comes from moving together with others. A third facet of body-based game design is the range of emotional transformations made possible by using the player's body to cultivate fantasy identity.

As we saw in chapters 1 and 2, avatars act as our prosthetic bodies in gameplay, providing us a vehicle for enacting fantasy roles alone and with others. Adding movement to a game can strengthen a player's identification with a character by leveraging physical enactment of the fantasy role of the avatar. For example, in *Star Wars: The Force Unleashed* (figure 3.4), players use physical movements to experience virtual power. They might pantomime picking up a heavy object and hurling it, while seeing an on-screen enemy flung through the air as a result. In this example, some of the emotion comes from the physical gesture itself, which signals strength and confidence, while some comes from the player's fantasy identification with the Jedi knight onscreen. The game's designers thus leverage signals from the player's own body to heighten the feeling of "really" being a Jedi—physically enacting a fantasy role and receiving visceral feedback that corroborates the fantasy.

In *Star Wars: The Force Unleashed*, on-screen cues reinforce the fantasy persona, as the enemy's body hurtles through the air, while digital images and sounds recreate the *Star Wars* universe.

But in recent years, game designers have also been experimenting with techniques and technologies for augmenting physical fantasy gameplay *without* screens and consoles. These games come in various subgenre flavors, including live action role-playing games (LARP), pervasive games, and augmented reality games.[36] LARPers physically enact fantasy situations together in real-world settings, typically with costumes and faux weapons. A precursor genre to modern digital role-playing games, LARP continues to be a thriving practice today in its own right (see, e.g., http://knutepunkt.org, the website for the annual Nordic LARP conference). Pervasive games also occur in real-world settings, with players moving across multiple locations as they play, while augmented reality games use technologies to reveal hidden information embedded in everyday objects chosen as game props; for example, players might hold a device over an object to read a hidden digital message. All three game communities have been at the vanguard of incorporating technology in ways that enhance the player/character's sensory and imaginative immersion in a fantasy game world.

For example, figure 3.16a, b shows a technology-enhanced glove, "the Thumin," created for an augmented reality game called *Momentum*. The Thumin allowed the player to look for hidden sources of magic. Rigged to identify RFID tags hidden in the landscape, the glove vibrated when stroked slowly over a surface where a tag, symbolizing "sources of mage," could be found. As the designers explain: "The act of stroking the physical surface of, e.g. a tree, while wearing a glove is authentic, even though the act invokes virtual content associated to the RFID tag. The act is focused on the tree rather than on the glove or the virtual content, and this is emphasized by the tangible

a

b

Figure 3.16a, b
The Thumin glove used RFID and vibrator technology to allow players of
an alternate reality game to search for "magic" objects.
Source: Momentum (The Interactive Institute, 2009)

feedback."[37] The deep integration of the device's form factor and sensory augmentations into the story world helps to transport players more wholly into the game and enhance the enactment of their game identities.

Wearables like the Thumin can also heighten players' social fantasy experience of a game. Figure 3.17a, b shows a gauntlet and backpack designed for a social movement-based game called *Hotaru* designed by Kaho Abe, my lab's artist in residence. This game explores the potential of costumes to be social game controllers.[38]

To play *Hotaru*, two players put on technology-enhanced costume elements—one wears a gauntlet and the other an energy tank (see figure 3.17). The players have complementary roles in the game; the player with the tank collects energy, and the player with the gauntlet releases the energy to battle an enemy. The two must hold hands to transfer the power between them. Inspired by the costume-based transformations from superhero shows like Kamen Riders,[39] in which gestures activate wearable technology to transform a person into a superhero, Abe designed *Hotaru* to draw on action poses and gestures. The players' coordinated movements, monitored and recorded by the costumes, leverage the physical feedback loop described earlier in this chapter. The game also incites emotional contagion, creating emotional responses and immersion among players and spectators. The costumes add to the sensory realism of the fantasy experience; the social game mechanics force interdependence; and the physical contact that happens when players hold hands to transfer energy heightens feelings of interconnection and intimacy. In many ways, *Hotaru* embodies most of the concepts discussed in this chapter and illuminates new possibilities for games in the future.

Figure 3.17a, b
Hotaru combines wearable technology and gameplay, to immerse players in fantasy personas.
Source: Hotaru: The Lightning Bug Game (Kaho Abe, 2015)

Wrapping Up

Our bodies dramatically shape our emotional experience. This is as true in gameplay as in real life. Thanks to the rise of movement-based game controllers and wearables, game designers can now use players' bodies themselves as a medium for shaping emotions and social connection. Through strategies requiring players to master fatigue or pain, to position their bodies in ways that evoke closeness and camaraderie, by challenging comfort zones and merging technology, reality and fantasy, game designers are innovating an ever richer emotional palette. Rather than immobilizing and devaluing the body, or isolating players from other people, games in the future have the potential to embrace and enhance the role of the body and movement in play. They may recouple the physical and emotional, gracefully augment and transform our social interactions, and support our performance of who we are, or who we want to be.

To be sure, it's also possible that these developments could lead in a different direction, further problematizing and fragmenting our understanding of what it means to be present with one another. Who is the real me and how do I interact? Who am I without my wearable augmentation and who am I to you if we are not engaging through technologically augmented roleplay? While these seem like new concerns, our society already confronts these questions every day, over more prosaic "technologies" such as makeup and clothing, as well as in the use of social media to manage social identity. Adding a layer of environmental responsiveness, and the dynamics of interpersonal interaction with and through augmentation technologies, will continue to challenge our ability to sort out all of these very human concerns.

4   Bridging Distance to Create Intimacy and Connection

When players in a room together laugh, jump, and tease each other, the power of games to drive connection, empathy, and closeness appears right before your eyes. Yet these days, some of the most memorable moments for players, times of quiet intimacy and deep friendship, happen without the in-person cues we usually rely on to build and convey emotional connection. An observer might never sense the emotional weight of these experiences that occur through networked gaming.

Ubiquitous connection has dramatically changed how we communicate with one another on a day-to-day basis, shaping how we understand community and copresence.[1] Texting, Twitter and Facebook, email, and blogs offer countless ways to check in on someone—or many someones. Game developers have interwoven networked communication and the sense of copresence it creates deep in the experiences that they offer players today. Though the media frequently cover changes in communication and social norms due to social media, they seem to rarely discuss or allow for the feelings and social interactions made possible by networked games. Game designers combine the building blocks of emotional connection described in chapter 2—coordinated action, avatar-based role-play—with the power of network connections to create a wide range of emotionally meaningful social experiences for players who are geographically distant from one another. In this chapter, I'll cover three examples of tactics game designers use: the sharing and exchanging of digital objects, the cultivation of "summer camp"–like contexts for play, and the shaping of hobbyist and activist communities around play.

A Note in Your Lunchbox

Human beings show and cultivate closeness with others through small everyday actions: putting a note or an extra treat in a child's lunchbox, leaving a sack of tomatoes from the garden on a neighbor's porch, setting out an item where it won't be forgotten in the morning for your partner, feeding the cat for a friend. Gift giving and favors are part of the social glue that holds us together and strengthens our connections with one another.[2] We also engage in other sorts of ongoing nonconversational exchanges that reveal who we are and how we feel about each other: playing a chess game by mail; keeping track of an old school friend through the extended social network, mass holiday letters, Facebook, and Google, punctuated by brief interactions at the occasional class reunion. These aren't conversation but they nevertheless strengthen the social fabric.

Digital games enhanced with network access can provide these sorts of social exchanges as part of the play experience. Consider, for example, *Words with Friends* (*WWF*) (see figure 4.1). This Scrabble-like game allows two people to compete for points as they fill a board with words. You can play with a friend in whatever turn rhythm works for each of you—you make a move, then when they make a move the app will let you know. There's

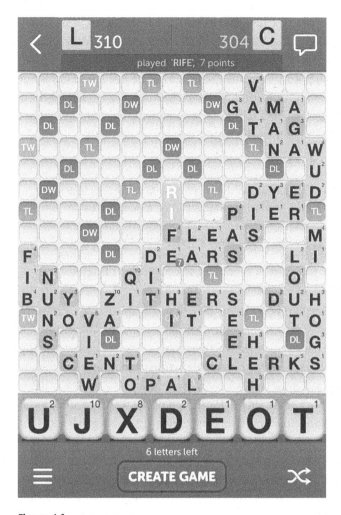

Figure 4.1

Words with Friends is a Scrabble-like game that can be played on a smartphone.

Source: Words with Friends (Zynga, 2015); screenshot courtesy of Luke Stark

no need to talk (though chat is an available feature) to see how things are going. The kinds of words you play and their values are a form of communication, as is the rhythm of play itself. Researcher Amy Bruckman reflected on the real-world impact of social connection through *Words with Friends*, explaining how Facebook matched her up for a game with her old high school friend Mike, whom she hadn't seen since the 1980s.

It felt great to reconnect with an old friend. . . . I would be inclined to dismiss the sense of connection as an illusion, except for one thing: Mike mentioned that next time I'm in New York I should look him up— we'll get coffee. The likelihood that I'll take him up on that invitation is fairly high. Before we played WWF, it wouldn't've crossed my mind. The chance of meeting up in person has gone from near zero to moderately high–a difference of multiple orders of magnitude. The real re-connection will take place in person. But it wouldn't have happened without the online connection.[3]

Games like *WWF* allow people to engage in a slow form of coexperience with enough expressive range to allow them to reveal themselves through their moves. Players enjoy weaving these interactions into the daily rhythm of computer and mobile phone use, which is generally more task-oriented. It's a light- weight way of keeping in touch, interwoven with existing social networking software that players might be using anyway—for example, *WWF* can be played through Facebook as well as on a mobile device as a standalone app. For a few moments here and there, these games can offer the feeling of sitting with a friend to play a hand of cards. They may not be enough to forge or sustain a tie on their own, but they do offer an access point and a kind of shared experience that can help strengthen a tie over time. Players express things about themselves as they strive to win, and competition provides spice as well as a frame for interaction.

Digital games with immersive fantasy worlds provide designers with additional tools for creating connection between players. In games where players need to acquire resources, equipment, and powers, for instance, gifting and sharing serve important social roles. For example, MMORPGs (massively multiplayer online role-playing games), like *City of Heroes*, discussed in chapter 2, allow players to give items to each other. These gifts may have practical value in the game, but they also express the gift giver's relationship to the recipient, and their own character, through what they give and when. Consider this post by a mother who plays *World of Warcraft* with her daughter:

> Would you call me a bad person if I confessed I couldn't actually recall the best gift I've ever been given in game? It was actually a whole set of items, though, and there's a reason I can't remember them either singly or as a unit. They're the quirky, humble gray and white items my daughter would wrap up and send me for the sheer delight of it when she first started playing confidently on her own. I have a whole row of these mementos in somebody or other's bank vault—flowers, low-level dresses, and odd gray drops that tickled her fancy when she came across them. I would know she had discovered something she loved when she would forbid me to walk behind her when she was at the keyboard, and I could clearly see that she was in town. She wrapped each gift with care, usually sending it along with a vendor-bought sweet treat if she had enough silver. None of these gifts were remarkable in and of themselves, but they were all so full of her joy of discovery and anticipation of sharing that nothing else I've ever been given can ever match them.[4]

Another example of the power of gifts comes from a game reporter given a preview of another acquisition-focused game, *Animal Crossing: New Leaf* (see figure 4.2a, b). In this game, the player visits with NPC townspeople and earns "bells" toward building out a home and its contents, as well as cultivating the general well-being of the town itself. Totilo received a tour of

a

b

Figure 4.2a, b
Animal Crossing: New Leaf is a game played on the Nintendo DS3 handheld console. The player homesteads in a town where she can become
mayor, interacting with inhabitant NPCs as well as other human players
who can visit her town using network capabilities.
Source: Animal Crossing: New Leaf (Nintendo, 2012); screenshot courtesy
of Kotaku (2013)

the game from co-creator Aya Kyogoku, in which he visited her town within the game:

Kyogoku directed me to some objects outside the train station. They were at my feet. "I left you some gifts," she said. There were baskets of fruit. There was a present wrapped in special wrapping paper. She encouraged me to open the gift. It contained carp streamers, a gift that only Japanese gamers were slated to receive from the game on Children's Day in early May. I'd never have unlocked it in my American copy of the game. . . . This wasn't a mere tour, obviously, it was a friendly sales pitch—with gifts. We all casually walked past a flag that just happened to have a *Kotaku* logo on it. Flattery! Later, they sent me a QR code to generate it.[5]

In this situation, the game's creators were using the emotional power of gifts to try to give the journalist a warmer feeling about the game. Later in the interview, Kyogoku invites him into her in-game 'home.' In writing about it, Totilo captures nicely the odd power of sharing in-game, and how it leaks into one's feelings:

We headed over to Kyogoku's primary home. She went inside. Eguchi stood by the mailbox. Just . . . go in? Yes, they told me. This was weird, maybe because I'm a mere *Animal Crossing* dabbler, maybe because this felt weirdly intimate. It felt different than hanging out outside in the virtual rain. Yes, we were playing a game. They were clearly trying to hype its features and generate a positive story. But I suddenly felt like I was imposing. Homes are private places. Walking into another person's— particularly that of a person who made the game—felt like a big step. Of course this wasn't really a home. I was just buying into the metaphor more strongly than I'd expected.

The charm of *Animal Crossing: New Leaf* is its combination of slow, thoughtful play in a magical little world, where you are usually alone but once in a while pass time with other players. Each day is different. The seasons change; the sun rises and sets, and the stars come out at night. In winter you may log onto the game and find it has snowed. NPC creatures and characters greet you and share the latest news. As one player puts it:

This is the crux of *Animal Crossing: New Leaf*'s genius. Rather than a game you may play intensely for a time and then finish, it is a much longer, slow unfolding experience. It draws you in day by day, until the first thing you do each morning is go and check on the prices of different fruit and see what your virtual friends have been up to. It's the closest thing I've come to a daily videogame meditation, at times it almost feels therapeutic—or maybe some strange experiment being carried out on the human race by Nintendo.[6]

The player's job in the game is to collect things as flora and fauna change with the seasons. Occasionally, you might invite others into the world and share its magic, just as you might bring a friend to a favorite spot in the country where you spent hours playing as a child. This kind of sharing is quite different from posting status updates and snapshots on social media, because it takes place within the context of the "magic circle" of gameplay. The magic circle is a term coined by Dutch historian and cultural theorist Johan Huizinga in the 1930s—a cocreated safe and bounded context in which players can comingle fantasy and reality, and which thus allows for freer and more flexible social connection and emotional expression.[7] To be invited into another player's own in-game home, and given a gift, provokes strong emotion, but also carries with it the safety of the magic circle of play, a charming and powerful combination.

Camp a Click Away

In chapter 2, we looked at social situations game designers craft for players, meant to cause certain kinds of social and emotional effects. For example, the game *Keep Me Occupied* was designed to heighten esprit de corps among activists at an Occupy camp in Oakland. The game's arcade machine, built to fit into a novel rearrangement of people in real time and space, emphasized their collective spirit and power. Networked game designers conjure virtual settings that feel like supercharged real-world places and use them to generate camaraderie among far-flung players. Stories of play in massively multiplayer online worlds can sound remarkably like anecdotes from mass gatherings in real life (albeit with fantastical elements). For example, in academic researcher Celia Pearce's account of her ethnographic work in an MMO called *There.com*, she describes a moment when players are engaged in a chaotic game, driving brightly colored buggies and chasing a ball, which she is trying to document for her research.

It's a little difficult to see in the midst of the buggy melee that is the playing field. So I hop off the buggy and don my hoverpack. I flit about in the air and take a load of pictures of the proceedings. The field is total bedlam. You can hear from the voice chat that group members are having a huge amount of fun.[8]

From her vantage point above the game, Pearce realizes that the ball has lodged itself high in a tree, and that her avatar, Artemesia, can get to it. As other players shout encouragement, she tries to knock the ball from the tree—and then finds herself sucked inside it.

At this point I stop taking pictures because I am too caught up in the moment (one of the hazards of playing and doing research at the same time), but I realized very quickly that the orb is driveable, so I use my arrow keys to roll it out of the tree back onto the playing field. With lots of shouting from the group, I find my way to the center of the field, position myself, take my hands off the arrow keys, and prepare myself for an all-out assault. It is in this way that I become the ball for the remainder of the Buggy Polo game.[9]

Pearce marks this moment as a turning point in her research, when she went from primarily observing to also engaging and actively participating. Transforming from an observer to an active and joyful participant might be familiar to anyone who ever went to summer camp. The camp experience works because of the setting and the activities that campers engage in together, which form a context for learning about oneself and bonding with others. Traditionally summer camps were set up in the wilderness, where campers would need to be more self-reliant in meeting everyday needs, and would explore a sometimes challenging environment together. The camp experience intentionally pushes campers out of their comfort zone, to engage them in mastery of new physical skills in the company of others, toward lifelong benefits.[10]

Game designers create a summer camp–like feeling for players through a combination of carefully wrought virtual worlds, game actions, and well-crafted avatars. Networked games allow players to explore unfamiliar and challenging terrain and to share their experience with other players. This shared online experience does the same kind of work as summer camp, encouraging personal growth in players and deepening their connections to one another. Game designers don't get enough credit for their skill in designing supportive environments for emotional and social growth.

The highly lauded indie game *Journey* (figure 4.3a, b) offers an elegant, pared-down example of the intentional design of collaborative exploration and discovery. Released in 2012, *Journey* won a wide array of game industry honors, including multiple BAFTA and Game Developers Choice awards. *Journey* was developed for the Sony PlayStation 3. As its name suggests, the game offers a journey through beautiful and challenging terrain, with

a

b

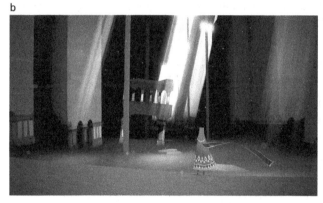

Figure 4.3a, b

Journey was designed to emphasize players' smallness in an awe-inspiring environment. Players engage in wordless collaboration to explore the game's terrain.

Source: Journey (thatgamecompany, 2012); *Journey* courtesy of Sony Computer Entertainment America LLC

a simple control scheme and set of player actions focused on traversing the landscape. *Journey's* lead designer, Jenova Chen, says he wanted to give players a "sense of small," like astronauts walking on the moon. Most games, he says, try to make players feel powerful by giving them magic, guns, and superpowers. Instead, Chen wanted players to experience awe at the game's majestic landscapes.[11]

The design choices in *Journey* all further this vision. The avatar in *Journey* is a small, simply robed figure, with a long flowing scarf (see figure 4.4). Unlike some of the games covered in chapter 1, *Journey* doesn't give players any choice in individualizing the avatar, although as players advance through the game, some subtle marks of experience appear on their avatars' cloaks. The diminutive avatar appears silhouetted against magnificent and sparse landscapes, all of which helps make the player feel tiny and insubstantial. The charm of operating the avatar lies in the magic of moving through the game landscape, and the fine-tuned responsiveness of both the avatar and the game world to the player's actions. Game reviewer Erik Kain says: "Even just sliding and floating down a huge corridor of flowing sand is a breathtaking experience, and being *in control* of how you make that descent causes it to be not merely a visual feast or something to observe, but something that is *actively fun to do.*"[12] Another reviewer says: "You have to press the X button for yourself and feel what it's like for your robed avatar to leave the desert floor and drift back down like a fallen leaf surfing a breeze. To play *Journey* is to savor the most incredible inner lightness. . . . To play *Journey* is to feel like a soul freed of its corporeal baggage."[13] This reviewer links the feeling of jumping in *Journey* to childhood fantasies of moonwalking:

Figure 4.4
Player characters jumping in *Journey*.
Source: Journey (thatgamecompany, 2012); *Journey* courtesy of Sony
Computer Entertainment America LLC

Kids don't dream of being astronauts in hopes of conducting tests on
mice aboard cramped space stations; they simply want to pogo around
on the moon. One giant leap, indeed. Followed by another, and another. Since most kids never get to realise this fantasy, we give them
inflatable Moonwalks at birthday parties and backyard trampolines to
soften the blow. And of course we give them videogames.[14]

Journey's enchanting gameplay and emotional appeal,
enhanced by an evocative musical score, seem naturally suited
to meditative, solitary play. But its designers also pushed the
boundaries of the multiplayer experience. Players can't do all
the game's activities or see all its wonders unless they sometimes
travel with others. Each player periodically finds another player
in the landscape who has been randomly paired with them over
the network. The designers chose a minimalist approach to crafting the communication possibilities between players; avatars can
only make a sort of chiming/chirping sound. They need to pay

close attention to each other and experiment with their actions to discover how to work together in the game. The wordless collaboration that takes place made for a powerful experience for one player:

This *reliance* on one another that's programmed into the game is what makes it so captivating. As I began to climb the final slopes and the wind and the dragons became more dire and my own situation more desperate, I found myself and this other anonymous person clinging to one another as we moved up the slope. When I was tossed aside by a dragon, left lying half-broken in the snow, the other traveler ran back for me. We climbed together. At this point, the idea of climbing alone had vanished from my thoughts entirely even though so often in games the solo route is the one I take. In a way that no other multiplayer game has done, I felt the *necessity* of companionship in *Journey*. In literally no MMO I've ever played have I felt that need, but in *Journey* that sense of struggle feeds directly into a sense of camaraderie. It's deeply affecting.[15]

Journey's designers use avatar visual design and physical responsiveness, vast and majestic landscapes and soundscapes, and powerful minimalist tools for coordinated action and communication to create a dramatic and transformative experience for players. Emotionally, playing the game evokes the sort of feelings that come up when sharing a challenging but temporary real-world adventure with someone, like a river rafting trip or summer camp outing. If you haven't played a networked game like this one, you should not underestimate how pleasant and "real" these experiences can be.

Collective Play as Community Builder

Journey's potent, stripped-down interdependence points to larger opportunities for game designers in networked multiplayer situations. Anytime players gather and take part in something that has a persistent alternate world, the stuff of their interaction can be shaped to create a positive experience. Players of games have always thrown their lot together to get further along, and also to enjoy the mutual pleasure of ruminating over and solving things among peers. With computers and the Internet, it's possible to make this happen at a mass scale.

Multiplayer networked games played in real time often require elaborate plans and communication among players through voice-based or text-based chat as players form raiding parties, launch attacks, and coordinate other in-game business. Massively multiplayer games bring hundreds of players together in much larger organized bodies such as guilds or factions that persist over months and years, developing their own social norms and lore. Designers have realized that extended play is far more meaningful when embedded in understandable human social frameworks for collective action.[16]

Players and scholars have written many perceptive pieces about the strong social and emotional ties formed by long-term play in persistent game worlds.[17] But few have explored the community-building capabilities of another kind of networked game—asynchronous mass play (players engaging in the same game at different times)—in games like *Words with Friends*. Spelling a word might be a solitary act, but players learn from each other's moves, enjoying the unique pleasure of tracing another person's thought process. In everyday life, we learn from observing one another, picking up nuances of practice so that we don't have to entirely reinvent the wheel each time we take up a new task.[18] Games at a mass scale allow us to observe one another's strategies and to create a community of expertise much as communities form around hobbies. With fishing, say, anglers enjoy solo trips, but they also enjoy planning trips with friends and strategizing with others, telling stories about their trips, and learning from each other's experiences. One of the deep pleasures of a hobby is the growth and strengthening of relationships around it. Networked games can tap into this same set of emotional and social pleasures, which are very different in quality than the pleasure of mass simultaneous action. They combine solitary joy with an appreciation of the expertise and knowledge of others. In some sense, perhaps, this is mass social gaming for introverts.

Joining in a fierce melee accompanied by frantic voice chat may not be my cup of tea, but I might genuinely enjoy the intellectual challenge and peer approval from a game called *Foldit* (see figure 4.5), where players try to "fold" new and more efficient protein structures. This game contributes to actual scientific research, helping scientists discover new proteins to fight diseases including HIV and cancer.[19] Researchers at the University of Washington designed and tuned the game so that laypeople could quickly master some fundamental strategies for protein folding, then begin to optimize structures on their own.

Foldit offers players a low-key, asynchronous, but still shared pleasure, enhanced by "coop-etition" encouraged by its reward system, providing rewards and motivations of many types. The designers included an overall leaderboard showing the top players, but also boards showing leaders in different puzzle types, for individuals playing alone and for groups working together. As the game's creators explain:

It's not just every person competing against every other person. There's a lot of social interaction that's supported by the game—chat and forums and things like that. Players can form teams to work together. So individual players can fold the protein for a little while, and then they can share that with other members of their group, who can pick up where they left off. The whole group gets credit for what the members have done, and the groups are competing against each other as well. The leaderboard system on the website is also meant to motivate people. We support different skill sets, rewarding and recognizing players for doing what they're good at.[20]

Top players of *Foldit* collaborate in teams but also do a lot of solo work, optimizing and tuning their protein structures, and

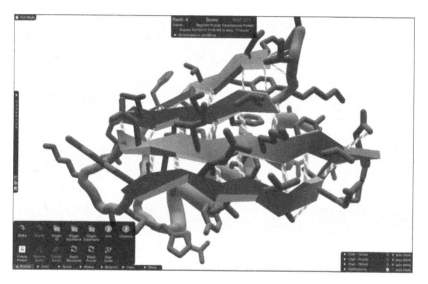

Figure 4.5
Foldit is a protein-folding game that provides real-world challenge problems to hobbyist gamers. Results of the efforts of players have been published in *Nature Biotechnology* (Christopher B. Eiben, Justin B. Siegel, Jacob B. Bale, Seth Cooper, Firas Khatib, Betty W. Shen, Foldit Players, Barry L. Stoddard, Zoran Popovic, and David Baker, "Increased Diels-Alderase Activity through Backbone Remodeling Guided by Foldit Players," *Nature Biotechnology* 30, no. 2 [2012]: 190–192, doi:10.1038/nbt.2109). *Source: Foldit* (Center for Game Science at University of Washington/UW Department of Biochemistry, 2013)

then comparing notes with teammates, sharing drafts that show their process. Some who were interviewed by Nature Video[21] report the rush they feel when they succeed in optimizing a structure. Says one: "When you've got it right, you see your protein moving and changing shape and your score rushes up, your own player name rushes up through the ranks, and your adrenaline starts." And another: "It's like being a scientist when you get your paper published. That 10 percent of euphoria is supposed to take you through that 90% of banging your head against the wall."

These players describe the joy of solo play that is carried out in the context of team challenges and contests set up by the researchers behind *Foldit*, which they know are linked to the potential for real scientific advances. The emotional payoff for them comes from being recognized for their efforts by the community as a whole, for something they deeply enjoy for personal reasons during moment-to-moment play. As one player puts it: "For me, it's a guilty pleasure, and yet here I am involved in something that has real relevance in the scientific world. It makes you proud of what you do, which is essentially a little hobby." *Foldit* adeptly combines the solitary pleasures of tinkering with the communal pleasures of valued contribution and demonstrated expertise. The scientists who created the game have clearly gained value from the player community, publishing results in journals including *Nature Biotechnology*.[22]

Wrapping Up

The widespread presence of network connections gives game designers a way to bring people together around shared emotional experience in play. Networked games often draw on activities of everyday life to strengthen ties—gift giving, sharing of hobbies and special hideaways, going "away" together in search of emotionally transformative shared experiences.

Of course there are drawbacks to creating such compelling social and emotional experiences at a distance. Unlike Hermione of the Harry Potter books with her time-turner that allows her to be in two places at once, each of us has only one continuous unfolding stream of time and attention. When we put our attention on something or someone who is far away using a networked device, it follows that we are not attending to what is copresent with us to the same degree. Amy Bruckman (the researcher quoted earlier discussing *Words with Friends*) eventually dropped the game for exactly this reason. She said that the game was "slowly taking over" her life. She describes how fitting the game into seemingly blank spaces in her day, like waiting to pick up her kids at school, wasn't as harmless as it seemed. Picking up her kids, she usually had a five-minute wait as they packed up:

So it's a perfect time to make my WWF move, right? Perfect except that if I'm playing a couple different games, I won't be done when they arrive. So I put away my phone, but part of my brain is still thinking about my move (what words end in "u"? "Tofu"? "Bayou"?) rather than paying full attention to what happened at school today. Until I finish making that move, I won't fully be there. And it's like that through my entire day. The little gaps I have don't match the amount of time it takes to make my WWF moves. The fact that you can play on your phone makes the temptation pervasive.[23]

The turn-taking and rhythms of connection in a networked game situation may not mesh well with the rhythms of interaction with people in one's "real-world" interactions. What do we do when these worlds collide? Which should have precedence?

And how do we navigate our feelings about the roles we play and the challenges we face in these various social settings? Is the fact that games provide a well-crafted, emotionally enriching, and socially empowering experience for players a potential hazard to their thriving in the more complicated, uneven, and nuanced real world? Or is this an underestimation of players' ability to self-regulate pleasures and responsibilities? Maybe it depends upon how busy their life is already.

Another hazard of network-enabled relationships: digital communities form in and depend upon fragile terrain. If a game no longer turns a profit, its creators may simply shut it down. Chapter 2 included anecdotes and reminiscences from players when *City of Heroes* shut down in 2012. Here is another player ruminating on this loss:

It's not like when they cancel a TV show, where you can still pull out the DVDs and enjoy it and share it with your friends who missed this beautiful gem when it was on the air. It's not like the awesome dark-horse of a game with the cancelled sequel. No, once the servers go down, the game is just fucking gone. I will never be able to play it again. I will never be able to show people the game, I will never be able to just fire it up out of nostalgia and give it a good play for old times' sake. This wasn't just a game for me, it was a *hobby*. It's something I put time into almost every week for eight years of my life. And it's just going to be fucking *gone*.[24]

Celia Pearce's book[25] traces a diaspora of players who met in an MMO called *Uru* that shut down and who wanted to preserve their community. Together, they recreated settings, costumes, and interactions from *Uru* in other MMO environments including *Second Life* and *There.com*. Amazed by the extent to which the players replicated areas of the original game, Pearce found the players' ongoing support of each other touching. MMO designers[26] note that many players recreate a certain character or persona for themselves again and again as they move from one MMO to another. Players also sometimes migrate (as the *Uru* players did) from MMO to MMO in groups, maintaining existing social networks in new contexts. Thus, in some sense, one's identity and relationships can survive these nomadic transitions from game world to game world.

Networked play experiences also allow for the kinds of flexible identity formation and experimentation discussed in chapter 2, which may inform real-world identity and relationship. Through these games, we may find "fellow travelers" helping us on our way through the game as well as our life challenges. As Turkle puts it:

Virtuality need not be a prison. It can be the raft, the ladder, the transitional space, the moratorium that is discarded after reaching greater freedom. We don't have to reject life on the screen, but we don't have to treat it as an alternative life either. We can use it as a space for growth. Having literally written our online personae into existence, we are in a position to be more aware of what we project in everyday life. Like the anthropologist returning home from a foreign culture, the voyager in virtuality can return to a real world better equipped to understand its artifices.[27]

Some believe the community and connections forged in networked play could be used to improve a wide range of nongaming contexts.[28] Whether or not this is so, gamers quoted in this chapter at least find networked social play deeply satisfying and enriching in and of itself. Network-enabled gaming has grown and coevolved alongside the rise of social software such as Facebook and Twitter, which some claim relates to the loss of "third places" in everyday life,[29] and the need for forming "social capital" nonetheless.[30] Scholars of play have always argued for the privileged place of play in social and emotional life[31] and even in the shaping of culture.[32]

Parents, teachers, communities, and social commentators have uneasily observed what seems to be the isolating, dividing effect of technology. And certainly we still need answers about the impact of networked games on children, adults, and communities. But if we all decide what we want games to do for our children and our society, then game designers hold unique tools for helping create subtle forms of connection and support.

In my view, these tools offer an antidote to some of our concerns about the ever-tightening weave of work, technology, leisure, and home life. Perhaps making virtual gifts in a networked game world for one's children and helping a stranger through an intimidating landscape are nurturing and loving experiences that can bring people together. In my opinion, we could be doing a lot worse things than "wasting" our time playing well-crafted games together.

Endgame: A Few Last Thoughts

I began this book with the claim that games have the capacity to take us into different emotional territory than any other medium. In the intervening four chapters, you've gotten a detailed look at specific design techniques in games that evoke strong emotions for individual players and also among people who play together. I've shown how astute design decisions, such as the amount of customization made possible in avatars and how they interact within a game world, can end up powerfully affecting how people connect and relate in the context of that game. We've seen how game designers make use of social signals and signifiers we know in "real life"—gift giving, going through risky situations together, physical closeness and contact, among others—to create strong feelings and connections between players as they engage the challenges of a game. If you were not already convinced, perhaps by now you will allow that games are an innovative medium that has a rightful place alongside the other media we value for their ability to reflect our own human experience back to us and for their capacity to take us into new emotional territory.

I used various analogies along the way—team sports, fishing, playing superheroes, taking care of a neighbor's pet—to help readers who don't play many games feel their way into this amazing aesthetic form. That's also one of the reasons why I drew most of my game examples from outside the mainstream of weapons and orcs and spaceships. Of course those games, too, carry great emotional power, and I mean no disrespect to the many game genres not covered here. However, one of my aims as a game researcher is to grow the emotional palette of games as we know them, and so I chose to pull examples from a wide territory within what is now known as gaming. Games are capable of so much, and there is room for a far broader range of thriving genres and forms than we have today. I hope the developers who read the book will be inspired to tinker and continue to evolve what they already do so well, to "change the dial" for the fun and inspiration of it, as Leigh Alexander puts it.[1]

Thank you for taking the time to read this small volume. By now you should have a more nuanced and detailed appreciation for how games move players emotionally that can be useful to you in understanding your own experience with games, and in thinking through what they may mean for you, and for those around you. Please use it as fodder for informed, nuanced conversations with other people who may or may not agree with your views about games, toward mutual enjoyment and illumination.

I want to close with an excerpt from one more game review (of *Journey*):

In a later part of the game, I found myself both exhausted and tested. What must the wanderer be going through right now, I wondered? Such pain, such hardship. At that moment, I thought back to the joyful beauty I had witnessed merely an hour ago—leaping through the sand, warm sun on my shoulders, the energy and freedom of youth urging me to jump higher, higher! And now here I was, head down, teeth gritted, pushing through the cold, bitter trials of adulthood. Those lost moments of grace felt fleeting even as they were happening, and they felt all the more fleeting in retrospect. But there was no way to get them back; nothing for it but to push onward. And so I did, and so you will too. And round and round we'll go.[2]

Notes

1   A Series of Interesting Choices

1. Alan Burdick, "Discover Interview: Will Wright," *Discover*, August 1, 2006, http://discovermagazine.com/2006/aug/willwright (accessed August 24, 2015).

2. Katie Salen and Eric Zimmerman, *Rules of Play: Game Design Fundamentals* (Cambridge, MA: MIT Press, 2004). Jesper Juul, *Half-Real: Video Games between Real Rules and Fictional Worlds* (Cambridge, MA: MIT Press, 2005).

3. Andrew Rollings and Dave Morris, *Game Architecture and Design* (Scottsdale, AZ: Coriolis, 2000).

4. Phoebe C. Ellsworth and Klaus Scherer, "Appraisal Processes in Emotion," in *Handbook of Affective Sciences* 572 (2003): V595.

5. Carien van Reekum, Tom Johnstone, Rainer Banse, Alexandre Etter, Thomas Wehrle, and Klaus Scherer, "Psychophysiological Responses to Appraisal Dimensions in a Computer Game," *Cognition and Emotion* 18, no. 5 (2004): 663–688.

6. Steven W. Cole, Daniel J. Yoo, and Brian Knutson, "Interactivity and Reward-Related Neural Activation during a Serious Videogame," *PLoS ONE* 7, no. 3 (2012): e33909, doi:10.1371/journal.pone.0033909.

7. Mihaly Csikszentmihalyi, *Finding Flow: The Psychology of Engagement with Everyday Life* (New York: Basic Books, 1997), 50.

8. Jenova Chen, "Flow in Games," MFA thesis, University of Southern California, 2006, http://www.jenovachen.com/flowingames/Flow_in _games_final.pdf (accessed August 24, 2015).

9. Nicole Lazzaro, "The Four Fun Keys," in *Game Usability: Advice from the Experts for Advancing the Player Experience*, ed. Katherine Isbister and Noah Schaffer (Burlington, MA: Morgan Kaufmann, 2008), 317–343.

10. http://chrishecker.com/Can_a_Computer_Make_You_Cry%3F (accessed August 24, 2015).

11. Richard Rouse, "Games on the Verge of a Nervous Breakdown: Emotional Content in Computer Games," *Computer Graphics* 35, no. 1 (February 2001), http://www.paranoidproductions.com/gamingandgraphics/ gg2_01.html (accessed August 24, 2015).

12. Donald Horton and Richard R. Wohl, "Mass Communication and Para-Social Interaction: Observations on Intimacy at a Distance," *Psychiatry* 19, no. 3 (1956): 215.

13. Lawrence W. Barsalou, "Grounded Cognition," *Annual Review of Psychology* 59 (2008): 617.

14. Burdick, "Discover Interview: Will Wright."

15. Miguel Sicart, "Defining Game Mechanics," *Game Studies* 8, no. 2 (December 2008), http://gamestudies.org/0802/articles/sicart (accessed August 24, 2015).

16. Heather Lee Logas, "Meta-Rules and Complicity in Brenda Brathwaite's Train," *Proceedings of DiGRA 2011 Conference: Think, Design, Play*, Utrecht, the Netherlands (2011), http://www.digra.org/wp-content/ uploads/digital-library/11301.05058.pdf (accessed August 24, 2015).

17. Jamin Brophy-Warren, "The Board Game No One Wants to Play More Than Once," Speakeasy, *The Wall Street Journal*, June 24, 2009, http://blogs.wsj.com/speakeasy/2009/06/24/can-you-make-a-board -game-about-the-holocaust-meet-train/ (accessed August 24, 2015).

18. Brenda Laurel, *Computers as Theatre* (Boston: Addison-Wesley Longman, 1991).

19. Katherine Isbister, *Better Game Characters by Design: A Psychological Approach* (Boca Raton, FL: CRC/Morgan Kaufmann, 2006).

20. http://www.reddit.com/r/truegaming/comments/242itf/first_person_vs_third_person_which_do_you_prefer/(accessed August 24, 2015).

21. Mathias Jansson, "Interview: Eddo Stern, Pioneer of Game Art," *Gamescenes: Art in the Age of Videogames*, June 12, 2010, http://www.gamescenes.org/2010/06/interview-eddo-stern.html (accessed August 24, 2015).

22. Regine, "Waco Resurrection," *We Make Money Not Art*, May 23, 2005, http://we-make-money-not-art.com/archives/2005/05/so-the-winners.php (accessed August 24, 2015).

23. Richard Hofmeier, *Cart Life*, http://www.richardhofmeier.com/cartlife/(accessed November 24, 2014).

24. Carolyn Petit, "Cart Life Review," *Gamespot*, January 14, 2013, http://www.gamespot.com/reviews/cart-life-review/1900-6402398/ (accessed August 26, 2015).

25. Ben Lee, "'Cart Life': How Richard Hofmeier Game Became a Success Story," Digital Spy, April 14, 2013, http://www.digitalspy.co.uk/gaming/news/a472874/cart-life-how-richard-hofmeier-game-became-a-success-story.html (accessed August 24, 2015).

26. Katherine Isbister, "Reading Personality in Onscreen Interactive Characters: An Examination of Social Psychological Principles of Consistency, Personality Match, and Situational Attribution Applied to Interaction with Characters," Ph.D. dissertation, Stanford University, 1998.

27. Katherine Isbister and Clifford Nass, "Consistency of Personality in Interactive Characters: Verbal Cues, Non-verbal Cues, and User Characteristics," *International Journal of Human–Computer Studies* 53, no. 2

(2000): 251–267. Byron Reeves and Clifford Nass, *The Media Equation* (Cambridge: Cambridge University Press, 1996).

28. Katherine Isbister, "The Real Story on Characters and Emotions: Taking It to the Streets," paper presented at Game Developers Conference 2008, San Francisco, California.

29. Monte Schultz, "Infocom Does It Again . . . and Again," *Creative Computing* (December 1983): 153.

30. Janet H. Murray, *Hamlet on the Holodeck: The Future of Narrative in Cyberspace* (Cambridge, MA: MIT Press), 52–53.

31. Ian Bogost, Simon Ferrari, and Bobby Schweizer, *Newsgames: Journalism at Play* (Cambridge, MA: MIT Press, 2010).

32. bluemist, "Love Plus: Impressions," *bluemist*, September 5, 2009, http://bluemist.animeblogger.net/archives/love-plus-1/ (accessed August 24, 2015).

33. Ibid.

34. Ibid.

35. Owen Good, "The One about the Guy Who Married a Video Game," *Kotaku*, November 21, 2009, http://kotaku.com/5409877/the-one-about -the-guy-who-married-a-video-game (accessed August 24, 2015).

36. Akiko Fujita, "On Vacation with a Virtual Girlfriend," *The Wall Street Journal*, web video, 3:13, August 31, 2010, http://www.wsj.com/ video/on-vacation-with-a-virtual-girlfriend/77E0EACD-0B57-49DD -876A-5FF74EFF0781.html (accessed August 24, 2015).

37. GodLen, "CNN Reports on the Love Plus Marriage," *Anime Vice*, December 17, 2009, http://www.animevice.com/news/cnn-reports-on- the-love-plus-marriage/3268/ (accessed August 24, 2015). Lisa Katayama, "Love in 2-D," *New York Times*, July 21, 2009, http://www .nytimes.com/2009/07/26/magazine/26FOB-2DLove-t.html ?pagewanted=1 (accessed August 24, 2015).

38. Katayama, "Love in 2-D."

39. Ibid.

40. Andrew Park, "The Sims Review," *Gamespot*, February 11, 2000, http://www.gamespot.com/reviews/the-sims-review/1900-2533406/ (accessed August 24, 2015).

41. Scott McCloud, *Understanding Comics: The Invisible Art* (New York: William Morrow, 1994).

42. shushbob, *Sims 3—Gameplay What Happens If You Fight*, YouTube video, 3:11, June 6, 2009, http://www.youtube.com/watch?v=1yexm4 JYhgY (accessed August 24, 2015).

43. Robin Burkinshaw, "Hello!," *Alice and Kev: The Story of Being Homeless in The Sims 3*, 2009, http://aliceandkev.wordpress.com (accessed August 24, 2015).

2 Social Play

1. Entertainment Software Association, "Essential Facts about the Computer and Video Game Industry," 2015, http://www.theesa .com/wp-content/uploads/2015/04/ESA-Essential-Facts-2015.pdf (accessed August 26, 2015).

2. Johan Huizenga, *Homo Ludens: A Study of the Play Element in Culture* (Boston, MA: Beacon Press, 1955).

3. Hara Estroff Morano, "The Dangers of Loneliness," *Psychology Today*, July 1, 2003, https://www.psychologytoday.com/articles/200308/the -dangers-loneliness (accessed August 26 2015).

4. Regan L. Mandryk and Kori M. Inkpen, "Physiological Indicators for the Evaluation of Co-Located Collaborative Play," *CSCW '04 Proceedings of the 2004 ACM Conference on Computer-Supported Cooperative Work*, Chicago, IL (2004): 102, doi:10.1145/1031607.1031625.

5. Anna Macaranas, Gina Venolia, Kori Inkpen, and John Tang, "Sharing Experiences over Video: Watching Video Programs Together at a Distance," *Human–Computer Interaction—INTERACT 2013*, Cape Town, South Africa (2013): 73–90.

6. Jaako Stenros, Janne Paavilainen, and Frans Mäyrä, "The Many Faces of Sociability and Social Play in Games," *Proceedings of the 13th International MindTrek Conference*, Tampere, Finland (2009): 82–89.

7. Kerry L. Marsh, Michael J. Richardson, and R. C. Schmidt, "Social Connection through Joint Action and Interpersonal Coordination," *Topics in Cognitive Science* 1, no. 2 (2009): 320, doi:10.1111/j.1756 -8765.2009.01022.x; Pierecarlo Valdesolo and David DeSteno, "Synchrony and the Social Tuning of Compassion," *Emotion* 11, no. 2 (2011): 262, doi: 10.1037/a0021302; Pierecarlo Valdesolo, Jennifer Ouyang, and David DeSteno, "The Rhythm of Joint Cction: Synchrony Promotes Cooperative Ability," *Journal of Experimental Social Psychology* 46, no. 4 (2010): 693, doi:10.1016/j.jesp.2010.03.004.

8. GameOn @ IGS Corporation Limited, *How to Control Sackboy: LBP2 Acting*, YouTube video, 1:50, October 21, 2011, https://www.youtube. com/watch?v=LHF7Psvu6GM (accessed August 26, 2015).

9. Brendan Keogh, "A Sackboy Says No Words," *Kill Screen*, March 15, 2011, http://killscreendaily.com/articles/sackboy-says-no-words/ (accessed August 26, 2015).

10. Ibid.

11. calculatorboyqwe, *New LittleBigPlanet Sackzilla Trailer HD Quality*, YouTube video, 1:48, September 3, 2008, https://www.youtube.com/ watch?v=xdvSAkgN-FU&feature=player_embedded (accessed August 26, 2015).

12. Erving Goffman, *The Presentation of Self in Everyday Life* (New York: Anchor Books, 1959).

13. D. Fox Harrell, *Phantasmal Media: An Approach to Imagination, Computation, and Expression* (Cambridge, MA: MIT Press, 2013).

14. Michael S. Rosenberg, "Virtual Reality: Reflections of Life, Dreams, and Technology: An Ethnography of a Computer Society," unpublished manuscript, 1992, https://w2.eff.org/Net_culture/MOO_MUD_IRC/ rosenberg_vr_reflections.paper (accessed March 26, 2015).

15. Quoted in Sherry Turkle, *Life on the Screen: Identity in the Age of the Internet* (New York: Simon & Schuster, 1995).

16. Ibid.

17. "Rip City of Heroes," *Penny Arcade*, August 2012, http://forums.penny-arcade.com/discussion/166289/rip-city-of-heroes (accessed January 31, 2015).

18. Ibid.

19. Ibid.

20. Ibid.

21. Ibid.

22. Ibid.

23. Ibid.

24. Walter Mischel, "Toward an Integrative Science of the Person," *Annual Review of Psychology* 55 (2004): 1–22.

25. Mary Flanagan, Daniel C. Howe, and Helen Nissenbaum, "Values at Play: Design Tradeoffs in Socially-Oriented Game Design," *CHI '05 Proceedings of the SIGCHI Conference on Human Factors in Computing Systems*, Portland, OR (2005): 751, doi:10.1145/1054972.1055076; Bernie DeKoven, *The Well-Played Game: A Playful Path to Wholeness* (Lincoln, NE: iUniverse, Inc., 2002).

26. "keep me occupied," *Auntie Pixelante*, January 9, 2012, http://www.auntiepixelante.com/?p=1461 (accessed August 26, 2015).

27. Espen Aarseth, "I Fought the Law: Transgressive Play and the Implied Player," *Proceedings of DiGRA 2007 Conference: Situated Play*, Tokyo, Japan (2007): 130, http://www.digra.org/wp-content/uploads/digital-library/07313.03489.pdf (accessed August 26, 2015); Mia Consalvo, *Cheating: Gaining Advantage in Videogames* (Cambridge, MA: MIT Press, 2009).

28. Raph Koster, "The Laws of Online World Design," *Raph Koster's Website*, http://www.raphkoster.com/gaming/laws.shtml (accessed January 31, 2015).

29. David Myers, *Play Redux: The Form of Computer Games* (Ann Arbor: University of Michigan Press, 2010).

30. Ibid.

31. Keogh, *A Sackboy Says No Words.*

32. Celia Pearce and Artemesia, *Communities of Play: Emergent Cultures in Multiplayer Games and Virtual Worlds* (Cambridge, MA: MIT Press, 2009), 216–217.

3   Bodies at Play

1. Roni Caryn Rabin, "The Hazards of the Couch," *New York Times,* January 12, 2011, http://well.blogs.nytimes.com/2011/01/12/the-hazards -of-the-couch/ (accessed August 26, 2015).

2. Katherine Isbister, "Emotion and Motion: Games as Inspiration for Shaping the Future of Interface," *Interactions* 18, no. 5 (September–October 2011): 24.

3. Katherine Isbister and Floyd 'Florian' Mueller, "Guidelines for the Design of Movement-Based Games and Their Relevance to HCI," *Human Computer Interaction* 30 (no. 3–4, 2015): 366–399; Elena Márquez Segura and Katherine Isbister, "Enabling Co-located Physical Social Play: A Framework for Design and Evaluation," in *Game User Experience Evaluation,* ed. Regina Bernhaupt (New York: Springer, 2015); Holly Robbins and Katherine Isbister, "Pixel Motion: A Surveillance Camera Enabled Public Digital Game," Katherine Isbister, "How to Stop Being a Buzzkill: Designing Yamove!, A Mobile Tech Mash-Up to Truly Augment Social Play," *MobileHCI '12 Proceedings of the 14th International Conference on Human–Computer Interaction with Mobile Devices and Services* (New York: ACM, 2012): 1–4; Isbister, "Emotion and Motion"; Katherine Isbister, Ulf Schwekendiek, and Jonathan Frye, "Wriggle: An Exploration of Emotional and Social Effects of Movement," *CHI '11 Extended Abstracts on Human Factors in Computing Systems* (New York: ACM, 2011), 1885–1890.

4. Fritz Strack, Leonard L. Martin, and Sabine Stepper, "Inhibiting and Facilitating Conditions of the Human Smile: A Nonobtrusive Test of the Facial Feedback Hypothesis," *Journal of Personality and Social Psychology* 54, no. 5 (1988): 768.

5. Dana R. Carney, Amy J. C. Cuddy, and Andy J. Yap, "Power Posing: Brief Nonverbal Displays Affect Neuroendrocrine Levels and Risk Tolerance," *Psychological Science* 21, no. 10 (2010): 1363.

6. Katherine Isbister, Rahul Rao, Ulf Schwekendiek, Elizabeth Hayward, and Jessamyn Lidasan, "Is More Movement Better? A Controlled Comparison of Movement-Based Games," *FDG '11 Proceedings of the 6th International Conference on Foundations of Digital Games 2011* (New York: ACM, 2011): 331.

7. Nadia Bianchi-Berthouze, Whan Woong Kim, and Darshak Patel, "Does Body Movement Engage You More in Digital Game Play? And Why?," *ACII '07 Proceedings of the 2nd International Conference on Affective Computing and Intelligent Interaction* (Heidelberg: Springer-Verlag, 2007): 102; Siân E. Lindley, James Le Couteur, and Nadia Bianchi-Berthouze, "Stirring Up Experience through Movement in Game Play: Effects on Engagement and Social Behavior," *CHI '08 Proceedings of the SIGCHI Conference on Human Factors in Computing Systems* (New York: ACM, 2008): 511; Isbister, Schwekendiek, and Frye, "Wriggle," 1885.

8. Katherine Isbister and Christopher DiMauro, "Waggling the Form Baton: Analyzing Body-Movement-Based Design Patterns in Nintendo Wii Games, Toward Innovation of New Possibilities for Social and Emotional Experience in Whole Body Interaction," in *Whole Body Interaction*, ed. David England (London: Springer-Verlag, 2011), 63; Katherine Isbister, Michael Karlesky, and Jonathan Frye, "Scoop! Using Movement to Reduce Math Anxiety and Affect Confidence," *CHI '12 Proceedings of the SIGCHI Conference on Human Factors in Computing Systems* (New York: ACM, 2012): 1075.

9. Elaine Hatfield, E., John T. Cacioppo, and Richard L. Rapson, *Emotional Contagion* (Cambridge, UK, and New York: Cambridge University Press, 1994).

10. Tom F. Price, Carly K. Peterson, and Eddie Harmon-Jones, "The Emotive Neuroscience of Embodiment," *Motivation and Emotion* 36, no. 1 (2012): 36, doi:10.1007/s11031-011-9258-1.

11. David A. Havas, Arthur M. Glenberg, Karol A. Gutowski, Mark J. Lucarelli, and Richard J. Davidson, "Cosmetic Use of Botulinum Toxin-A Affects Processing of Emotional Language," *Psychological Science* 21, no. 7 (July 2010): 895–900.

12. Dean Tate and Matt Boch, "Break It Down! How Harmonix and Kinect Taught the World to Dance; The Design Process and Philosophy of *Dance Central*," Game Developers Conference 2011, http://www.gdcvault.com/play/1014487/Break-It-Down-How-Harmonix (accessed August 26, 2015).

13. Gina Kolata, "Yes, Running Can Make You High," *New York Times*, March 27, 2008, http://www.nytimes.com/2008/03/27/health/nutrition/27best.html (accessed August 26, 2015).

14. Florian "Floyd" Mueller, Frank Vetere, Martin R. Gibbs, Darren Edge, Stefan Agamanolis, Jennifer G. Sheridan, and Jeffrey Heer, "Balancing Exertion Experiences," *CHI '12 Proceedings of the SIGCHI Conference on Human Factors in Computing Systems* (New York: ACM, 2012); Isbister and Mueller, "Guidelines for the Design of Movement-Based Games and Their Relevance to HCI."

15. Sm00t, "I Lost 70 Pounds Entirely Playing Dance Dance Revolution and Have since Gained 25 Pounds of Muscle and Growing," */r/IAmA Reddit Driven Q&A*, July 8, 2012, http://www.topiama.com/r/106/i-lost-70-pounds-entirely-playing-dance-dance (accessed August 26, 2015); Associated Press, "Video Game Fans Dance Off Extra Pounds," *DNITech*, May 24, 2004, http://www.dnitech.com/danceoffthepounds.htm (accessed August 26, 2015).

16. Alexander Sliwinski, "West Virginia University Study Says DDR Helps Fitness Attitude," *Joystiq*, December 21, 2006, http://www.engadget.com/2006/12/21/west-virginia-university-study-says-ddr-helps-fitness-attitude/ (accessed August 26, 2015).

17. http://www.immersence.com/osmose/ (accessed August 26, 2015).

18. Joe Donnelly, "Experiencing 'Deep', the Virtual Reality Game That Relieves Anxiety Attacks," *Vice* (2015). http://www.vice.com/en_uk/read/experiencing-deep-the-virtual-reality-game-that-relieves-anxiety-attacks-142 (accessed August 26, 2015).

19. Simon Parkin, "Desert Bus: The Very Worst Video Game Ever Created," *The New Yorker,* July 9, 2013, http://www.newyorker.com/tech/elements/desert-bus-the-very-worst-video-game-ever-created (accessed August 26, 2015).

20. Ibid.

21. Ibid.

22. http://www.pippinbarr.com/games/dmai/ (accessed August 26, 2015).

23. See http://eddostern.com/works/tekken-torture-tournament/ (accessed August 26, 2015).

24. *Pong* is an early computer game that simulates paddle tennis.

25. See Simgallery.net.

26. Kerry L. Marsh, Michael J. Richardson, and R. C. Schmidt, "Social Connection through Joint Action and Interpersonal Coordination," *Topics in Cognitive Science* 1, no. 2 (2009): 320, doi:10.1111/j.1756-8765.2009.01022.x; Pierecarlo Valdesolo and David DeSteno, "Synchrony and the Social Tuning of Compassion," *Emotion* 11, no. 2 (2011): 262, doi: 10.1037/a0021302; Pierecarlo Valdesolo, Jennifer Ouyang, and David DeSteno, "The Rhythm of Joint Action: Synchrony Promotes Cooperative Ability," *Journal of Experimental Social Psychology* 46, no. 4 (2010): 693, doi:10.1016/j.jesp.2010.03.004.

27. Edward T. Hall, "Proxemics," *Current Anthropology* 9, no. 2–3 (1968): 83; Mark L. Knapp and Judith A. Hall, *Nonverbal Communication in Human Interaction,* 3rd ed. (New York: Holt, Rinehart & Winston, 2002).

28. Douglas Wilson, "Designing for the Pleasures of Disputation—or—How to make friends by trying to kick them!," Ph.D. dissertation, IT University of Copenhagen, 2012, http://doougle.net/phd/Designing_for_the_Pleasures_of_Disputation.pdf (accessed August 26, 2015).

29. See http://www.nslgames.com (accessed August 26, 2015).

30. Christopher Cole Gorney, "Hip Hop Dance: Performance, Style and Competition," MFA thesis, 1977, Department of Dance, University of Oregon.

31. Kerry L. Marsh, Michael J. Richardson, and R. C. Schmidt, "Social Connection through Joint Action and Interpersonal Coordination," *Topics in Cognitive Science* 1, no. 2 (2009): 320, doi:10.1111/j.1756-8765.2009.01022.x; Pierecarlo Valdesolo and David DeSteno, "Synchrony and the Social Tuning of Compassion," *Emotion* 11, no. 2 (2011): 262, doi: 10.1037/a0021302; Pierecarlo Valdesolo, Jennifer Ouyang, and David DeSteno, "The Rhythm of Joint Action: Synchrony Promotes Cooperative Ability," *Journal of Experimental Social Psychology* 46, no. 4 (2010): 693, doi:10.1016/j.jesp.2010.03.004.

32. Isbister, "How to Stop Being a Buzzkill," 1.

33. Pierecarlo Valdesolo and David DeSteno, "Synchrony and the social tuning of compassion," *Emotion* 11, no. 2 (2011): 262, doi: 10.1037/a0021302; Pierecarlo Valdesolo, Jennifer Ouyang, and David DeSteno, "The Rhythm of Joint Action: Synchrony Promotes Cooperative Ability," *Journal of Experimental Social Psychology* 46, no. 4 (2010): 693, doi:10.1016/j.jesp.2010.03.004.

34. See http://ninjashadowwarrior.tumblr.com (accessed August 26, 2015).

35. Holly Robbins and Katherine Isbister, "Pixel Motion: A Surveillance Camera Enabled Public Digital Game," *Proceedings of Foundations of Digital Games 2014*, Fort Lauderdale, FL (2014), http://www.fdg2014.org/proceedings.html (accessed August 26, 2015).

36. Annika Waern, Markus Montola, and Jaakko Stenros, "The Three-Sixty Illusion: Designing for Immersion in Pervasive Games," *CHI '09 Proceedings of the SIGCHI Conference on Human Factors in Computing Systems* (New York: ACM, 2009): 1549, doi:10.1145/1518701.1518939.

37. Ibid.

38. Jason Johnson, "Are Costumes the New Game Controllers?," *Kill Screen*, July 12, 2013, http://killscreendaily.com/articles/are-costumes-new-game-controllers/ (accessed August 26, 2015);Katherine Isbister and Kaho Abe, "Costumes as Game Controllers: An Exploration of Wearables to Suit Social Play," paper presented at the 9th International

Conference on Tangible, Embedded and Embodied Interaction, Stanford, CA (2015).

39. https://www.youtube.com/watch?v=T3zGRmVES0w (accessed August 26, 2015).

4 Bridging Distance to Create Intimacy and Connection

1. Howard Rheingold, *Smart Mobs: The Next Social Revolution* (New York: Basic Books, 2003); Clay Shirky, *Here Comes Everybody: The Power of Organizing without Organizations* (New York: Penguin Books 2009); Amy Jo Kim, *Community Building on the Web: Secret Strategies for Successful Online Communities* (Berkeley, CA: Peachpit Press, 2000).

2. Marcel Mauss, *The Gift: Forms and Functions of Exchange in Archaic Societies*, trans. Ian Cunnison (New York: Norton Library, 1967); John F. Sherry, "Gift-Giving in Anthropological Perspective," *Journal of Consumer Research* 10, no. 2 (1983): 157.

3. Amy Bruckman, "Reconnecting with Old Friends Online—Is the Sense of Connection an Illusion?," *The Next Bison: Social Computing and Culture* (blog), April 2, 2013, https://nextbison.wordpress.com/2013/04/02/reconnecting-with-old-friends-online-is-the-sense-of-connection-an-illusion/ (accessed August 27, 2015).

4. Lisa Poisso, "Breakfast Topic: What's the Best In-Game Gift You've Ever Received?," *WoW Insider*, October 6, 2012, http://www.engadget.com/2012/10/06/breakfast-topic-whats-the-best-in-game-gift-youve-ever-receiv/ (accessed August 27, 2015).

5. Stephen Totilo, "I Played the New Animal Crossing with the People Who Made It," *Kotaku*, June 8, 2013, http://www.kotaku.com.au/2013/06/i-played-the-new-animal-crossing-with-the-people-who-made-it/ (accessed August 27, 2015).

6. Andy Robertson, "Animal Crossing New Leaf Creates a Living Breathing World," *HuffPost Tech: UK*, May 17, 2013, http://www.huffingtonpost.co.uk/andy-robertson/animal-crossing-new-leaf-creates-living-breathing-world_b_3291549.html (accessed August 27, 2015).

7. Johan Huizinga, *Homo Ludens: A Study of the Play-Element in Culture* (Boston: Beacon Press, 1955).

8. Celia Pearce and Artemesia, *Communities of Play: Emergent Cultures in Multiplayer Games and Virtual Worlds* (Cambridge, MA: MIT Press, 2009).

9. Ibid.

10. Michael D. Eisner, *Camp* (New York: Warner Books, 2005).

11. Kevin VanOrd, "Journey Impressions," *Gamespot*, June 17, 2010, http://www.gamespot.com/articles/journey-impressions/1100-6266636/ (accessed August 27, 2015).

12. Erik Kain, "'Journey' Review: Making Games Beautiful," *Forbes*, December 4, 2012, http://www.forbes.com/sites/erikkain/2012/12/04/journey-review-making-video-games-beautiful/ (accessed August 27, 2015).

13. Jason Killingsworth, "The Edge ExPlay Panel: Journey—How Jumping Can Be Emotional," *Edge*, November 5, 2012, https://web.archive.org/web/20121108054721/http://www.edge-online.com/features/opinion-designing-rapture%E2%80%A8%E2%80%A8 (accessed August 27, 2015).

14. Ibid.

15. Kain, "'Journey' Review."

16. Kim, *Community Building on the Web*; Raph Koster, "The Laws of Online World Design," *Raph Koster's Website*, http://www.raphkoster.com/gaming/laws.shtml (accessed January 31, 2015).

17. Pearce and Artemesia, *Communities of Play*; T. L. Taylor, *Play between Worlds: Exploring Online Game Culture* (Cambridge, MA: MIT Press, 2009).

18. Albert Bandura, *Social Learning Theory* (New York: Pearson, 1976).

19. Seth Cooper and Katie Burke, "Behind the Scenes of Foldit: Pioneering Science Gamification," *American Scientist*, 2013, http://www.americanscientist.org/science/pub/behind-the-scenes-of-foldit-pioneering-science-gamification (accessed February 2, 2015).

20. Cooper and Burke, "Behind the Scenes of Foldit."

21. https://www.youtube.com/watch?v=axN0xdhznhY (accessed August 27, 2015).

22. Christopher B. Eiben, Justin B. Siegel, Jacob B. Bale, Seth Cooper, Firas Khatib, Betty W. Shen, Foldit Players, Barry L. Stoddard, Zoran Popovic, and David Baker, "Increased Diels-Alderase Activity through Backbone Remodeling Guided by Foldit Players," *Nature Biotechnology* 30, no. 2 (2012): 190–192, doi:10.1038/nbt.2109.

23. Amy Bruckman, "A Great Experience That Must Stop: Words with Friends and the Mindful Use of Technology," *The Next Bison: Social Computing and Culture* (blog), April 6, 2013, https://nextbison.wordpress.com/2013/04/06/a-great-experience-that-must-stop-words-with-friends-and-the-mindful-use-of-technology/ (accessed August 27, 2015).

24. "Rip City of Heroes," *Penny Arcade*, http://forums.penny-arcade.com/discussion/166289/rip-city-of-heroes (accessed January 31, 2015).

25. Pearce and Artemesia, *Communities of Play*.

26. Koster, "The Laws of Online World Design."

27. Sherry Turkle, *Life on the Screen: Identity in the Age of the Internet* (New York: Simon & Schuster, 1995).

28. Jane McGonigal, *Reality Is Broken: Why Games Make Us Better and How They Can Change the World* (New York: Penguin Books, 2011); James Gee, *The Anti-Education Era: Creating Smarter Students through Digital Learning* (New York: Palgrave Macmillan, 2013).

29. Ray Oldenburg, *The Great Good Place* (New York: Paragon Books, 1989).

30. Robert D. Putnam, *Bowling Alone: The Collapse and Revival of American Community* (New York: Touchstone Books, 2000).

31. Mihaly Csikzentmihalyi, "Play and Intrinsic Rewards," *Journal of Humanistic Psychology* 15, no. 3 (1975): 41.

32. Huizinga, *Homo Ludens*.

Endgame

1. Leigh Alexander, "Grunge, Grrrls and Video Games: Turning the Dial for a More Meaningful Culture," *Gamasutra*, August 16, 2013, http://www.gamasutra.com/view/feature/198376/grunge_grrrls_and_video_games_.php (accessed August 27, 2015).

2. Kirk Hamilton, "*Journey*: The Kotaku Review," Reviews, *Kotaku*, March 1, 2012, http://kotaku.com/5889425/journey-the-kotaku-review (accessed August 27, 2015).

Ludography

Abe, Kaho, *Hit Me!* (Kaho Abe, 2011)

Abe, Kaho, *Hotaru: The Lightning Bug Game* (Kaho Abe, 2015)

Abe, Kaho, *Ninja Shadow Warrior* (Kaho Abe, 2011)

Antonisse, Jamie, and Devon Johnson, *Hush* (freeware, 2008)

Antropy, Anna, *Keep Me Occupied* (freeware, 2012)

Baker, David, *Foldit* (Center for Game Science at University of Washington/UW Department of Biochemistry, 2013)

Blackman, Haden, *Star Wars: The Force Unleashed* (LucasArts, 2008)

Chen, Jenova, *Journey* (thatgamecompany, 2012)

Chopra, Deepak, *Leela* (THQ, 2011)

Eguchi, Katsuya, and Kiyoshi Mizuki, *Wii Sports* (Nintendo, 2006)

Hofmeier, Richard, *Cart Life* (freeware, 2011)

Jillette, Penn, *Penn and Teller's Smoke and Mirrors* (including *Desert Bus*) (Absolute Entertainment, 1995)

Meretsky, Steve, *Planetfall* (Infocom, 1983)

Morawe, Volker, and Tilman Reiff, *PainStation* ("//////////fur//// art entertainment interfaces," 2001)

Moro, Isao, and Aya Kyogoku, *Animal Crossing: New Leaf* (Nintendo, 2012)

NYU Game Innovation Lab, *Pixel Motion* (2013)

NYU Game Innovation Lab, *Yamove!* (2012)

Romero, Brenda, *Train* (exhibited only, 2009)

Stern, Eddo, *Waco Resurrection* (c-level, 2004)

Uncredited, *Black and White: Creature Isle* (Lionhead Studios, 2002)

Uncredited, *Bounden* (Game Oven, 2014)

Uncredited, *City of Heroes* (Cryptic Studies, 2004)

Uncredited, *Dance Central* (Harmonix, 2010)

Uncredited, *Dance Dance Revolution* (Konami, 1998)

Uncredited, *Little Big Planet 2* (MediaMolecule, 2011)

Uncredited, *Love Plus 3DS* (Otaku Gaming/Konami, 2009)

Uncredited, *Tekken* (Bandai Namco Entertainment, 1994)

Uncredited, *There.com* (Makena Technologies, 2003)

Uncredited, *Words with Friends* (Zynga, 2015)

Uncredited, *World of Warcraft* (Blizzard Entertainment, 2004)

Waern, Annika, Markus Montola, and Jaakko Stenros, *Momentum* (The Interactive Institute, 2006)

Wilson, Douglas, Brent Knepper, and Sara Bobo, *J. S. Joust* (Die Gute Fabrik, 2014)

Wright, Will, *The Sims 3* (Electronic Arts, 2009)

Wright, Will, *The Sims* (Electronic Arts, 2000)

Index